Fontana Introduction to Modern Economics
General Editor: **C. D. Harbury**

Each of the seven books in the series introduces the reader to a major area or aspect of modern economics. Each stands on its own, but all fit together to form an introductory course which covers most A-Level and first-year university syllabuses, and those of most professional bodies.

*An Introduction to Economic Behaviour*, by C. D. Harbury, Professor of Economics, City University.

*Private and Public Finance*, by G. H. Peters, Professor of Economics, University of Liverpool.

*Income, Spending and the Price Level*, by A. G. Ford, Professor of Economics, University of Warwick.

*Economics of the Market*, by G. Hewitt, formerly Lecturer at the Civil Service College.

*International Trade and the Balance of Payments*, by H. Katrak, Lecturer in Economics, University of Surrey.

*Britain and the World Economy, 1919–1970*, by L. J. Williams, Senior Lecturer in Economics, University College of Wales, Aberystwyth.

*Mathematics for Modern Economics*, by R. Morley, Lecturer in Economics, University of Durham.

# C. D. Harbury

*Professor of Economics, the City University*

# An Introduction to Economic Behaviour

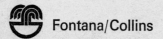 Fontana/Collins

First published in Fontana 1971
Reprinted October 1973
Third Impression September 1975

Copyright © C. D. Harbury 1971

Printed in Great Britain
for the Publishers Wm. Collins Sons & Co Ltd.
14 St James's Place, London, S.W.1,
by Richard Clay (The Chaucer Press), Ltd,
Bungay, Suffolk

# Contents

Introduction

# An Approach to Economics

This introductory book provides a broad basis for the understanding of economic behaviour. As described on the inside cover, it is the opening volume of a series which covers a first year course in modern economics for sixth forms, undergraduates, and students taking professional examinations; but the reader who wants to deepen his understanding of society rather than to undertake a systematic study of economics will find that the approach to the subject followed here will suit his purpose too.

The book does not deal with all the formal trappings of economic analysis, but it does give the newcomer to the subject the chance to handle many of the most important of them. It is designed to give the reader something of a feeling for the subject, to set him properly in the ways of thought of economists, and to prepare him for more systematic treatment in later volumes in the series.

The ordering of the subject matter is a little unusual. Indeed if I were reviewing this book, my first reaction might be to quarrel about it. But economics is not a subject with a beginning and a natural development. There is no generally accepted way of building up the subject from logical beginnings. The order chosen depends upon the needs of the particular reader, and that adopted here reflects my desire to relate economics to experience, both direct and indirect, through general reading. But it is a good idea to read the book right through from cover to cover, without pausing too long over any difficult passages, in order to obtain a feeling for the nature of economics. The reader may then, with benefit, return to particular sections that require closer study.

The first three chapters provide an overview of the economic system. They are followed by two chapters dealing with the analysis of the functioning of the price mechanism in different kinds of market. Emphasis is then switched to the behaviour of the economy seen as a whole—the area known as macroeconomics. Chapter 8 is devoted to questions of policy, and contains an analysis of the case for and against intervention in the functioning of free markets.

Finally, Chapter 9 is a long postscript which deals with the methods of economics. Introductory textbooks conventionally put this material much earlier. Experience, however, suggests that premature treatment of 'scope and methods' is both boring and largely meaningless before a student has done some work in the subject. I have, therefore, relegated the discussion of methods of analysis to the end of the book, so that the student may relate it to what he has learned about what economists do. There is no reason, however, why a teacher should not assign Chapter 9, or parts of it, to be read earlier. In particular, the reader who is not completely sure of the proper way to use and interpret graphs, should certainly refer to the Appendix, as soon as he finds any difficulty in understanding the diagrams used liberally throughout the book.

# Chapter 1

# The Family Budget

---

On average, families in London spend about 50 per cent more on housing than families in the rest of the country. Not, on the face of it, the most inspiring piece of information with which to start a book on economics. Yet it is a matter which bristles with exciting implications for an economist.

Why, one may wonder, should the Londoner spend nearly £4·75 per week on providing a roof over his head, while his provincial neighbour spends only about £3?[1] What reasons can be put forward to explain this fact, which on reflection turns out to be rather less immediately obvious than it might have seemed at first sight?

There are many possible explanations. The difference has almost certainly something to do with the price of houses in London relative to those in other places. But that is not in any real sense a basic explanation. It simply begs the question *why* prices of houses in London are relatively high. Not everything else is dearer in London.

What then is the full explanation? Has it anything to do with high costs of production, including the price of land? Are Londoners richer than other people so that they can afford to pay higher rents? If so, is it because they actually earn more, or because they can more easily economise on other things, such as fuel, since the weather happens to be warmer than in Scotland for example? Alternatively, do Londoners simply like good housing relatively more than other things, such as good eating and drinking, so that their larger housing expenditure is, rather, a reflection of their different tastes? Whatever the explanation, we can be fairly sure that it is not a simple one, but is likely to be a combination of many complex factors, including some of those already mentioned, as well as others.

The unravelling of interrelationships of this kind, identifying all the important causal links, is a part of the job of the economist,

1. The figures relate to the year 1969, which were the most recent available when this book was written. You might find it worth while to have a look at more recent data. The source is an annual publication, given at the foot of Table 1.1

though he often has to call upon other social scientists to help him, as we shall see in the last chapter of the book.

Family expenditure on housing, however, is only a single example of one kind of economic behaviour, and economic behaviour is what the economist tries to analyse. Attention was focused on housing expenditure because it happens to show some rather dramatic regional variations. Let us widen our view, for a moment, and look at the pattern of total household expenditure in Britain.

Table 1.1   **Family expenditure, 1969**
*Average weekly expenditure of all households*

|  | *Pounds* | *Per cent of total* |
| --- | --- | --- |
| Housing | 3·27 | 12·4 |
| Fuel, light, and power | 1·74 | 6·6 |
| Food | 6·89 | 26·1 |
| Alcoholic drink and tobacco | 2·48 | 9·4 |
| Clothing and footwear | 2·34 | 8·9 |
| Durable household goods | 1·66 | 6·3 |
| Other goods | 1·91 | 7·2 |
| Transport and vehicles | 3·67 | 13·9 |
| Services | 2·34 | 8·9 |
| Miscellaneous | ·08 | ·3 |
| Total | 26·38 | 100% |

Source: Department of Employment and Productivity. *Family Expenditure Survey 1969.* (H.M.S.O., London 1970) (Note: To be precise the survey deals with households—a term used as a strict definition of the vague notion of a family. For further information see the original.)

Table 1.1 is based on information supplied by about 10,000 families, and shows how total spending was divided between various goods and services in 1969. In that year, average weekly household income was about £32·50 of which some £6 was taken up by income tax, national insurance contributions, and savings of one sort or another. The remainder—£26·38—was spent on 'goods' and 'services'. A little more than a quarter of this total went on food, and another quarter on housing, durable household goods, such as furniture and electrical appliances, and on fuel. About a tenth of total expenditure, as shown in the table, was spent on alcoholic drink and tobacco, although it is well known that people consistently understate their true expenditure on these items (on alcoholic drink by about a half, and on tobacco by about a quarter). The remaining items call for two comments. First, that 'other goods' comprises all products not in previous categories, and includes such things as books, cameras, cosmetics, medicines, pets, and toys. Secondly, there is the group described as 'services'. This is the name given to items of expenditure which are made, not in order to acquire a tangible good, but for the performing of some service. We obtain a service when, for example, someone entertains us at the theatre or cinema, when someone tries to cure us of a disease, to teach us economics, or to repair our old alarm clock.

## Explaining consumer behaviour

The bare outline of the pattern of household expenditure in the last paragraph throws no light on the *causes* of consumer behaviour, which were claimed to be a concern of economists. At this stage of our study of economics, we are not going to be able to identify all the reasons why people spend their income in the way that they do. We can however suggest what some of these reasons may be. Table 1.2, for instance, highlights one of the most interesting of all to the economist—variations in income.

Table 1.2   **Family expenditure by household income, 1969**
*Per cent of total weekly expenditure on goods and services*

|  | Weekly income of household | | | |
| --- | --- | --- | --- | --- |
|  | Under £6 | £15 but under £20 | £30 but under £35 | £60 or more |
|  | % | % | % | % |
| Housing | 18·1 | 15·0 | 11·7 | 10·2 |
| Fuel, light, and power | 14·1 | 8·0 | 6·4 | 4·6 |
| Food | 30·4 | 29·1 | 26·4 | 20·8 |
| Alcoholic drink and tobacco | 5·1 | 9·4 | 9·8 | 9·5 |
| Clothing and footwear | 5·2 | 7·5 | 8·7 | 10·1 |
| Durable household goods | 5·5 | 5·6 | 6·0 | 7·7 |
| Transport and vehicles | 8·6 | 9·9 | 15·7 | 17·8 |
| Services | 7·1 | 8·1 | 8·5 | 11·8 |
| Other | 5·7 | 7·2 | 6·9 | 7·1 |
| Total | 100% | 100% | 100% | 100% |

Source: As for Table 1.1 (Note: Totals may not add to exactly 100 per cent because of rounding.)

## Income as a determinant of consumption

Table 1.2 shows the way in which households with different incomes allocate their expenditure over the same categories of goods and services as Table 1.1. It is a simplified version of the full survey from which it is taken, but two of the four income groups included are reasonably representative of the poor (incomes of less than £6 per week), and the relatively affluent (incomes of £60 or more per week). Two intermediate ranges of income are also shown, £15 to £20 and £30 to £35.

Study of Table 1.1 suggests that there are a number of different kinds of relationship between household income and consumption expenditure, and it will be useful to classify goods on the basis of these relationships. In the first place we may distinguish two fairly obvious categories—(i) those goods where expenditure falls *relative to income* as income increases, and which therefore absorb a smaller proportion of total expenditure at high than at low incomes, and (ii) those goods which are relatively more important when incomes are high.

i. *Goods which absorb a decreasing proportion of total expenditure as income rises.* The most famous of these products is food. As can be seen from Table 1.1 expenditure on food accounts for nearly a third of total spending of the poorest group, but only about a fifth of that of the highest income class. The German statistician Ernst Engel drew attention in the last century to the tendency for expenditure on food to fall proportionately as income rises, and it is sometimes known as Engel's law. Expenditure on housing and fuel and light is in the same category, and it is tempting to call all these products 'necessities'. But the word has, unfortunately, no easily recognisable meaning, because what is really essential to life forms only a very small part of the whole.

Necessities include items which are necessary not to sustain life itself, but to sustain life at a socially acceptable level. Once this view is admitted, it becomes hard to find an objective standard by which to judge whether any particular thing should or should not be classed as a 'necessity'. It becomes rather a question of personal opinion. To a conventional middle class clerk, necessities probably include at least one suit and a radio, if not a television set. To a hippie, or even a teacher, such things may well not be considered necessities. So, in order to avoid considerations of personal taste, economists prefer to put goods into categories according to which they may be easily and clearly recognised. One such category includes products which absorb a decreasing proportion of expenditure as income rises.

ii. *Goods which absorb an increasing proportion of total expenditure as income rises.* The opposite kind of relationship exists where a commodity becomes relatively more important at high incomes than at low. Table 1.1 suggests that clothing and durable household goods may be in this category, but among the most widely recognised is the group known as services, which includes entertainments, holiday expenses, hairdressing, etc.

For similar reasons to those which were advanced in discussing necessities, we would be wise to resist the temptation to describe these things as luxuries, for one man's luxury is another man's necessity, to twist a cliché. It is better to stick to an objective definition of goods and services such as that based upon whether expenditure on them rises (as a proportion of the total) as income increases. Many things commonly and loosely described as luxuries are properly included in this class.

Finally, we should note an omission. One of the most important ways of disposing of income does not appear here at all, namely saving, i.e. not spending on any goods or services. Saving does not show up in the figures presented in Tables 1.1 and 1.2, because these are confined to actual expenditure. However, there is a pronounced tendency for the proportion of income saved to be greater among the rich than among the poor, for the obvious reason that the latter need to spend most, if not all, their income simply in order to live. We shall return to consider the implications of this matter in Chapter 7. A major part of economic theory is closely related to it.

## Other relationships between income and expenditure

Within each of the nine or ten groups of goods and services used in Tables 1.1 and 1.2 are many hundreds, if not thousands, of different items. Because of this simplification, certain important relationships between income and expenditure have not shown up in Table 1.2. In particular we may mention two:

i. *Goods the consumption of which is absolutely less at high incomes than at low.* Such goods are given a special name in economics— **inferior goods.**[2] By this is meant no more than that they behave in the

2. See below Chapter 4, p. 57 for a further discussion of inferior goods. Note that we cannot use the information in Table 1.2 to identify inferior goods because the figures there are *proportions* of total expenditure, not *absolute* quantities purchased.

manner just described. Inferior does not imply anything else in an absolute sense, but the sort of goods which qualify are those which people find become less desirable than others when their income rises.

Potatoes are sometimes thought to be in this category, as the poor may be expected to eat more of them than the rich, who can afford to eat meat, which they obviously prefer. Incidentally, the evidence of the family expenditure surveys does not support this fact for present-day Britain, even though expenditure on potatoes does appear to rise only relatively slowly with income. They belong therefore in our major class (ii) above, rather than in this one.

A better example of an inferior good is fish and chips. There is a clear tendency for total expenditure at the fish and chip shop to decline in absolute terms as we go up the household income scale above £35 to £40 per week. Presumably this is because higher income groups use other cafés and restaurants instead. Another example, more surprising perhaps, occurs in the case of certain solid fuels, consumption of which is less in some higher income brackets than in lower ones. This is presumably a reflection of the fact that people who can afford more modern and expensive forms of heating, such as gas, electricity, and even oil, prefer it substantially to coal.

ii. *Goods on which consumption expenditure is proportional to income.* These demonstrate another consequence of lumping so many individual goods and services into a small number of classes; it conceals the existence of many goods which are consumed roughly in proportion to income. Even in Table 1.1 we can observe some goods and services which are of this nature over a fair range of incomes, if not over all. Alcoholic drink and tobacco, for instance, take very similar proportions of total expenditure for three of our four income classes; and even durable household goods, which we previously put in our major class (ii) (increasing), do not rise very substantially in relative importance over the lowest income groups.

### Consumption determinants, other than income

It has been suggested that changes in the level of household income are associated with different purchasing habits for certain kinds of goods and services, but it must be obvious that income is not the only determinant of consumption behaviour. Some other probable influences are manifested in Figure 1.1. For instance, large families tend to spend relatively less on housing themselves than do small

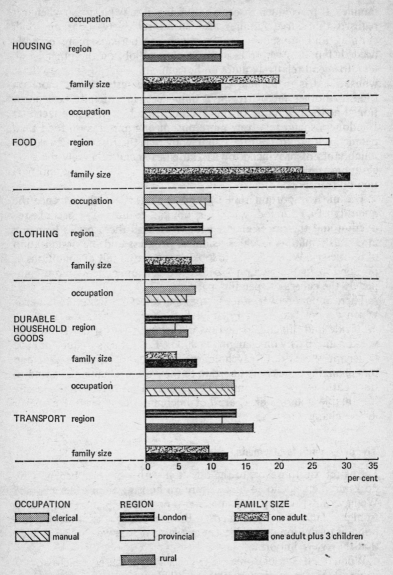

*Figure 1.1* Family expenditure by occupation of head of household by region and by family size 1969. (Per cent of total weekly expenditure on selected goods and services.) Source: as for Table 1.1

families. If this tendency seems surprising, it may be less so when it is realised that large families also spend relatively more on food, clothing and household goods, which are perhaps more urgently needed. Families whose head has a clerical job, on the other hand, tend to spend relatively more on housing and clothing than do those whose head is in manual employment. The latter spend more on food. Another factor, regional influences, has already been mentioned at the beginning of this chapter. In addition to the fact that Londoners spend relatively more on housing and less on food than people in other areas of the country, there is the further fact that the inhabitants of provincial towns and cities spend relatively more on clothing, while those who live in the country spend a higher proportion on transport.

The most important single group of factors which influence the quantity of a commodity which is bought, relate to its costs of production and the prices charged for it. Behind these prices lie many more basic matters, such as technical progress and the organisation of businesses. We shall have to look later more closely at conditions of production in the economy before we can understand more completely the causes of spending patterns.

There are, moreover, some factors that affect consumption patterns which do not feature in Figure 1.1. Some, like climate and tastes, are fickle and difficult to tie down. Tastes are based partly on convention and partly on changing fashions. Economists frequently have to rely on the work of psychologists and sociologists when they find that changing tastes are important to their work. Changing consumption patterns, which cannot be explained by other more easily identifiable determinants, are not uncommonly described as being due to changes in taste.

## The determinants of housing expenditure

Let us return, however, to the question with which we began. Why do Londoners spend so much more on housing than other people? We have already suggested one or two possible explanations, related to higher land and building costs. But we would need a lot of additional information not at present available before we could conclude that they were important.

What, then, about some of the other hypotheses which we advanced? As far as the importance of higher income is concerned, we can offer some observations. True, average household income in London is significantly higher than outside it (rather more than 10 per cent), but, while this can help to explain greater absolute housing expenditure, the conclusion we drew from Table 1.1, about the relationship between housing expenditure and income, leads us to doubt whether it is a good explanation of the greater relative expenditure of Londoners.

What else can the data which we have looked at suggest? Referring again to Figure 1.1 it will be remembered that we observed that relatively large housing expenditure seems to be associated with two other household characteristics—clerical rather than manual occupations and small rather than large families. Moreover, there do happen to be relatively more clerks than factory workers in the capital, and the number of children per London household is also lower than in any other major region in the country.

These facts can be no more than suggestive. It would be entirely unwarranted to pretend that we have provided even part of the explanation of our particular puzzle. It seems likely that higher housing expenditure by Londoners is related to all of the factors mentioned— to higher incomes, smaller families, more white collar workers, and higher house prices in the capital. But we cannot even be sure whether these are responsible, let alone estimate their relative quantitative importance; and there are surely several other factors involved, such as the influence of government policy on rent control.

The entire business of identifying the causes of economic behaviour is a very complex one. It involves the use of advanced statistical techniques, which by no means always lead to definite conclusions. Because of this, there are some economists who would consider it dangerous and misleading to suggest that any light at all can be thrown on the subject by the simple kind of analysis which we have been able to perform at this stage of our study of the subject.

There is some truth in this argument. The reason we have not been greatly influenced by it is that we are not primarily concerned here with the question of explaining any particular aspects of consumer behaviour. Our concern with housing expenditure has been simply to illustrate the kind of problem that interests economists. If any reader were to think that we have offered much by way of contribution to the understanding of the causes of expenditure patterns for real products, then we must quickly disillusion him.

To return for the last time to the reasons for the higher housing expenditure by Londoners, however, one final point may usefully be made. Expenditure on housing depends not only on consumer preferences, but also on the number of houses available in different parts of the country. This in turn depends on the stock of old houses in existence, and on the costs of producing new ones. Goods and services that people want do not fall from the skies like rain. They have to be produced at some cost in terms of the resources needed for their production. We must, therefore, turn now to examine the relation between outputs of goods and inputs of resources.

# Chapter 2

# The Business of Production

---

When we discussed, in the previous chapter, the question of how families decide to distribute their expenditure on the various goods and services that they consume, we conveniently ignored the fact that all the food, clothing, household goods, and other things have to be produced before anyone can buy them.

We now turn to examine this production side, and the way in which decisions are taken in institutions which we shall describe as businesses. There are a number of important considerations about the nature of business decision-taking which must be taken into account.

i. Businesses, in contrast to households, have three rather than one kind of decision to make. Each firm must make up its mind *what* to produce from all the goods and services of which it is capable, *how much* to produce of each item, and *how*, i.e. in what manner to produce it. The last question involves a choice of techniques, of how to combine resources, such as labour, machinery, land, and raw materials, in the productive process. Commonly, there are a number of alternative ways in which a good can be produced. In agriculture, for instance, cereals and vegetables may be grown in many different ways, each using varied proportions of labour, land, fertiliser, tractors, etc. (differing factor 'mixes'). A farm's efficiency may well reflect the particular factor combination that the farmer chooses to employ.

ii. Businesses are entities whose internal organisation must influence the production decisions they make. There are many distinctive forms of business organisation—ranging from the small one-man firm to the giant multi-product company—and each tends to have its own way of reaching decisions. Moreover, businesses have a number of goals, or objectives, which they may try to achieve. We shall discuss these in more detail later in this chapter. However, we may already observe that one common business objective is to try to make profits. Indeed, much economic analysis is based upon the assumption that firms try to **maximise** their **profits**. We need not question the validity of this assumption now, for there is no doubt that the profit motive influences businesses in the decisions that they have to make about the production of goods and services.

iii. Businesses must take account of their external economic environment, which limits the range of possible courses of action open to them. In the first place, a business is obviously affected by considerations of production costs which are influenced, in turn, by the availability and prices of the resources it needs to employ, and by known techniques of production. Secondly, business decisions on what to produce depend on the characteristics of the markets in which they operate. A firm which sells goods in a highly competitive market, for instance, probably has a good deal less choice about the price it can charge than another firm which sells a unique article or service for which few, if any, substitutes exist.

## Types of goods and services

We shall be able to appreciate the reasons for business decision-taking more easily if we illustrate our discussion by reference to specific goods and services. But a contrast must be made with household decision-taking. The classification of commodities which we adopted for analysing consumer expenditure in Chapter 1 (food, clothing, household durables, etc.) turns out to be less helpful when looked at from the point of view of a business.

Consider, for a moment, the basis on which our classification for household decision-taking rests. In analysing consumer expenditure, what we did was to employ a criterion of the use to which a good or service is put. Why did we do this? In a sense the notion of use might be completely arbitrary. There is nothing of any absolute value in the idea of the use to which a good is put. Yet we allocated all expenditure aimed at purchasing something for people to wear to a category called clothing, and all products which are for eating we class as food. Why did we not group products together according to colour, size, shape, or weight, for example? Red cheeses have a common characteristic with red hats. Cars and elephants resemble each other more closely in weight than do cars and bicycles. So do footballs and some round Dutch cheeses, and there are other criteria which could form the basis for quite different subdivisions of items.

The answer to the question of why we based our analysis of spending behaviour by households on the use to which goods and services are normally put is that it helped us to understand the reasons for consumer behaviour. The classification proved useful because people buy things because of the use that they can get from them. When considering whether to buy a ball point pen or a pencil, for instance, we tend to think of these items as **substitutes** which have very similar uses. That is why we adopt the use basis for our analysis of consumer behaviour.

Consider now the major decision-making unit that we are currently concerned with—businesses. How helpful is the use criterion in understanding their behaviour? The answer is not yes or no, but a qualified admission that it might be useful. Think for a moment about what we wish to explain. Instead of asking whether a family will buy beef or lamb, we want to ask whether a business will produce for sale beef or lamb. Is this, in fact, the relevant choice facing it?

The answer to this question depends on two factors: the kind of business we are interested in and the kind of good the firm produces. If, for instance, we wish to understand the behaviour of retail shops, our use criterion will be quite appropriate. Shops are commonly organised for the sale of goods used for the same general purposes. There are food stores, clothing shops, sweet shops, pet shops, restaurants, public houses, etc., each selling something designed to satisfy a particular want or purpose—eating, dressing, drinking, etc.

But if we are interested, as we certainly ought as economists to be, not only in the retail sale of goods but also in their production, the matter may well be different. Only may be, not necessarily will be. In the example we started with, beef and lamb, the same category happens still to be a useful one. The producer here is a farmer. He may truly have the choice of producing either lamb or beef as he considers whether to pasture sheep or cattle. On the other hand, the real alternatives facing him may be basically different. If, for example, the climate happens to be suitable for sheep but not for cattle, then the choice which a farmer has may not be whether to keep cows or sheep, but whether to graze a flock of sheep principally *for their meat or for their wool*. Then he would be on the margin between producing something for one use, food, or for another very different use, clothing. In this case our use criterion is not nearly so helpful.

### Industry groups

What alternative basis might prove more satisfactory? One good answer rests on the fact that a wide range of business behaviour is not so much use- (or product-) oriented as **process-oriented**. In manufacturing business, for example, it is common to find firms which are skilled in a particular production process, but whose products happen to cover a range of different uses. A task like the welding of steel tubes, for example, can be relatively easily adapted to the production of chair frames, or of car roof racks, as well as of many other things.

A foundry can cast a block for a sewing machine, a motor car engine, or a lamp-post, but the uses of these products bear remarkably little resemblance to each other. Or, to give a last illustration, the processes of spinning and weaving natural fibres into cloth are sensibly kept together regardless of whether material is to be used for clothing, furnishings, or sails for fishing boats. It is true that production techniques differ radically for some new artificial fibres, which are made in complicated chemical operations. But this only underlines the point that the relevant criterion for classifying goods from the viewpoint of discussing how businesses make decisions about what to produce must be an operationally useful one. Nylon manufacture may be better considered part of the chemical industry than of the textile industry. And many of the most convenient categories are process-based, like engineering, metal manufacture, mining, etc.

Bearing in mind the need to have an operationally helpful framework within which to analyse business behaviour, we may now examine further the influence exerted in a business by the internal and external factors mentioned earlier.

## Business organisation

We have already stressed the importance of profits as a prime goal of business activity. Although a firm will not necessarily act with profit maximisation in mind in the short run, it may well have to do so in the long run if it is not to be forced out of business.

There are, however, other targets at which a business may aim. These include maximising growth or sales, or securing a quiet life for the managers. In connection with the last of these, we may note as a relevant matter the nature of the legal form of business known as a joint stock company. Most large and medium, and very many small firms in Britain are organised as companies, mainly because this form of organisation makes it much easier for them to borrow money to expand. A joint stock company raises capital by issuing, or selling, shares in the business, which carry the right to receive future profits in return for cash.[1] Persons buying shares become shareholders, and they are the true owners of the business. However, shareholders do

1. See G. H. Peters, *Private and Public Finance*, Chapter 7, in this series for a more detailed treatment of the forms of business organisation.

not control the detailed policy of their companies. Instead they appoint directors whom they hope will act in their interests. The control that shareholders have over directors rarely extends beyond the power to appoint, reappoint, or sack them. This power is exercised at company general meetings. As a rule, such meetings are only conducted annually, after the directors have issued a report and a set of accounts on the previous year's trading.

In theory, shareholders are always in a position to remove unsatisfactory directors. But in very large companies where there are thousands of individual small shareholders, none of whom has a very large shareholding and few of whom bother to attend or vote at the annual general meeting, it is very difficult for enough of them to get together to exercise effective control. In such companies the directors are not, in practice, necessarily influenced by the shareholders very much. While the latter may be keenest on policies to maximise profits, the directors may be more interested in other objectives, such as those mentioned above, which may make life more agreeable for themselves. In cases where companies are director-dominated, profit maximisation may not be the primary goal at which the firm is aiming, at least in the short run.

**External influences—costs and markets**

With a given form of internal organisation, the decisions taken by a business on what, how much, and how to produce are greatly influenced by two sets of factors external to it—those affecting costs of production, and those relating to the market in which it sells.

*Costs of production*

Production costs for a business depend upon the availability of resources, including their prices, and the skill and efficiency with which they are used in the production process. These resources, or inputs, are known as the **factors of production**. There are many ways of classifying them, but it is common to group them according to the characteristics that they possess. The traditional division of factors of production distinguishes **labour, land** and **capital**, with a fourth factor, **enterprise**, sometimes separated from the rest.

i. *Labour*. The distinguishing feature of this factor of production is that it provides a human service which can be employed in most production processes. The reward, or price, that labour receives for this service is called a **wage**. Wages are associated with labour's productivity, and productivity depends on a variety of matters, such as the training and education which a particular worker has received, his innate skill, and the extent to which he is, or is not, motivated to give his best effort in the job he is doing. Hence, the businessman has to decide not only how much labour to hire, but he also has a choice of what kind of labour to employ—how much skilled, semi-skilled, and unskilled.

The efficiency of the labour force is also connected, from the viewpoint of society as a whole, with matters such as the size, sex, age, and geographical distribution of the population and with any relevant national characteristics. Finally, to avoid any confusion, it should be emphasised that it is the *services* of labour which are sold by an individual to a business. Labour itself would only be sold in a society which practised slavery.

ii. *Land and natural resources.* This group of inputs represents what might be called the gifts of nature, the naturally fertile land in the world, the fish in the sea, the heat of the sun that helps to dry grapes and change them into raisins, the rain that helps farmers everywhere grow their crops, the mineral wealth below the surface of the earth, etc. The income received by land is known as rent. A word of warning should be added here that in everyday speech the word rent is often used in quite a different sense to mean the charge made to someone for borrowing or hiring anything from a car to a flat. Moreover, economists employ the term **economic rent** in a highly specific sense, which will be examined later.[1] We may, however, point out that rent is commonly paid for something more than the use of land or another natural resource, but includes also an element of payment for another factor which is involved in making a resource available in a useful form. The labour which assists in the process of bringing minerals to the surface is a fair example. Iron ore is of no use while it is still in the ground. Land, too, increases in productivity and value if it is improved with fertilisers, irrigation, and the erection of fences and buildings. So 'rent' paid for this kind of fertile land is rather a mixed sort of factor reward.

iii. *Capital.* The third major factor of production, capital, consists of outputs of man-made goods such as machinery, factory and office equipment, industrial buildings, lorries, etc., which raise the productivity of other factors. It is not always easy, in practice, to draw a clear distinction between capital and other factors of production. For instance, expenditure on education may be considered as

2. See Chapter 5, pp. 81–85.

capital investment, since it tends to raise the productivity of labour. Hence, when a firm hires a skilled worker, it is really buying some 'embodied' capital as well as pure brawn. Capital is, however, traditionally distinguished, in principle, from both labour and land (which are sometimes referred to as primary factors) because it is an output of one industry and an input of another.

The productivity of a business is related to the quality of its capital as well as to the quantity. Old machines are often replaced by new larger and better ones. It is of great interest to know how much an increase in efficiency depends upon a rise in the quantity of capital employed, and how much on the technical progress implied in the development of an improved machine; but in practice this, too, turns out to be difficult to measure at all precisely.

The earnings of capital, the price that has to be paid for it, are known as **interest**, which is usually stated as a rate per cent, representing the sum paid by a borrower who needs finance to purchase a piece of capital equipment.

iv. *Enterprise.* A fourth factor of production, **enterprise**, is sometimes distinguished in economics. This is a highly artificial concept, introduced in order to be able to give a name to a single factor which might be said to receive the residual **profits** of a business after all other costs of production have been covered. Profit is said to be the reward for bearing the **risk** of organising production of a novel kind. When a totally new product, such as a three-dimensional encyclopedia for example, is being contemplated, or a company wants to start drilling for oil in an area where none has been found before, some one, or group of, persons has to put up the finance before the operation can get off the ground. If there is no way of estimating the probable success of the project except by intuition or guesswork, then any financial return on the investment would be pure profit.

The risk involved in some large capital investments is sometimes so great that no private individuals are prepared to take it. Governments may then step in, as they did with the Concorde airliner. In other cases, the hope of high profit may secure the necessary investment, especially since there have grown over the years ways and means of reducing business risks, such as by pooling them. But if the risks are reduced, the return on investment begins to assume the nature of interest rather than of pure profit. This illustrates one of the greatest difficulties of trying to pretend that there is a single separate factor of production which undertakes the risks of new investments. We cannot, in practice, identify any actual persons whose income is 'pure' profit. The problem is, however, a general one and is not confined to the factor enterprise. Only on rare occasions can a particular person be associated with a single type of factor income. It is more sensible to think of an individual receiving some part of his income in the form of a wage or salary, a part as interest on invested capital, and so on, as appropriate.

## Factor combination and efficiency

Our understanding of the nature of the factors of production leads us to consider the question of the manner in which they are used by a business. We have already pointed out that there is usually more than one possible manner of combining inputs in order to produce a given output. Consider, for instance, alternative labour and capital combinations in a single factory which makes toffees. Several methods of production may be used, one of which economises more on labour, another on capital. For toffee wrapping and packing may be done in several different ways—entirely by hand, by machines which need the attention of operatives for manual loading, or by a completely automatic machine.

The choice between different combinations of factor inputs depends on their relative efficiencies, the size of desired output, and the price of each factor service. There is nothing special to be added at this stage about factor prices, although we shall return to this subject in Chapter 5. The size of desired output is clearly important. It would obviously be uneconomic to use a very expensive piece of capital equipment unless the quantity of product justified it. You do not find blast furnaces in garages, although there are occasional jobs they would be useful for. To put the matter differently, it may be said that there may be a best or **optimum** scale of output for a firm, with given capital equipment.

The potential efficiency of each factor is usually accepted by economists as a technical datum, or a psychological one perhaps, in the case of labour. The productivity of a factor, however, is also related to the number of tasks it is expected to perform. The fewer they are (i.e. *the more specialised* the factor) the more productive that factor is likely to be. Almost any modern factory illustrates the point in countless ways, although it was emphasised by Adam Smith in his book *The Wealth of Nations* as long ago as 1776. Take a car assembly line for example. Each individual worker on the line has a limited range of jobs. One puts in the rear lights, another the instrument panel, a third the floor covering, and so on. And it must be patently obvious that the daily output of assembled cars can be maintained with many fewer workers than if each man tried to assemble a complete car himself.

It is hardly necessary to ask why. It is easier for a man to acquire a single skill than to acquire several, and skill and dexterity increase with repetition. Time is saved moving from task to task. Equipment is used economically. Instead of every man having a complete set of tools—hammer, screwdriver, pliers, etc.,—he needs only the specific tool required for his particular job. Additionally, we may observe that specialisation stimulates mechanisation since it raises the level of output of a particular process. And, as was argued above, it only becomes worth while to use some expensive, complex piece of machinery if the load justifies it. So, while it may not pay to have a single costly and complicated machine for the entire car assembly operation, it may be sensible to equip one man with a highly specialised power tool, rather than give all men a complete set of hand tools.

In this connection, what are called the 'social' costs of specialisation in factories should be mentioned—the boring routine of a single task repeated hour after hour, week after week, year after year, so dramatically and comically portrayed by Chaplin in his classic film, 'Modern Times'. While, however, we may deplore some of the humanitarian consequences arising from the proliferation of boring work, the benefits of large outputs have been very great indeed. There is no doubt that specialisation between individuals, between firms, and even between nations, has in no small measure been responsible for raising material living standards from the relatively low levels of the pre-industrial era.

## Market considerations

The second set of external factors which may influence a firm's production decisions are related to the characteristics of the **markets** in which it has to operate.

Economists find it useful to distinguish between market situations according to the extent to which the individual firm has power to exert control over its market. We should not be surprised to find that this power depends on such matters as the size of the firm relative to total consumer demand for the product, how far the firm sells a product which is highly individualistic (described as **differentiated** from the products of its competitors) and whether or not new firms are relatively free to enter the industry. It is obvious that these matters affect a firms power to manoeuvre: by, for instance, changing its selling price without adversely affecting its sales. Whether a market is, in fact, highly competitive or is more inclined to be monopolistic, is a subject to which we shall return in Chapter 5.

We may, however, already observe that the degree of competition in a market can affect the internal organization of a firm. For example, on the question raised earlier—whether businesses try to maximise their profits—we may reasonably infer that the extent to which a firm (even if it is director-dominated) has a real choice between trying to maximise profits and seeking a more modest return may depend on its power to influence the market for its product. In a highly competitive situation, with profits tending to be generally on the low side, a failure to maximise profits may simply mean bankruptcy. But a powerful company in a monopolistic position may be able to sit back without trying to extract the highest possible profit, if an 'adequate' level can be achieved with relatively little effort.

There is one final point to be added. Market considerations are important not only for the market in which a firm sells its product (which has been discussed in the previous paragraph) but also for the market in which it buys the services of factors of production. Hence, we may expect that the most efficient combinations of factors of production for a firm may not be the same if it is unable to influence their prices, as if it is in a partial monopoly situation where, for instance it is so large an employer of a particular kind of labour that it is forced to pay higher wages if it wishes to take on more men.

### The interdependence of production decisions

We are almost ready to link the subject-matter of this chapter with that of the last, by examining the way in which the decisions of businesses on production and the decisions of households on consumption are brought into line with each other. First, however, we must recognise that production decisions in one industry are not independent of those in another. Some businesses, as we know, do not sell their products direct to households at all. They manufacture goods, like capital equipment, which are **inputs** for other businesses. And there are industries, such as the car industry, which sell part of their **output** to final consumers, and part to other businesses for use in their productive processes.

The interdependence of sectors of the economy upon each other may be illustrated by means of a table, known as an **input–output table**.

*An input–output table*

Let us suppose that we have a very simple economy in which there is only one primary factor of production. We can imagine it to be labour, supplied by households. Next, let us assume that there are only two industries, which we shall call agriculture and clothing. Both industries supply goods to households for final consumption but, in addition, each sells some output to the other industry for use as an input. This may seem reasonable enough if clothing output is

Table 2.1 **Input–output table for a hypothetical economy[3]** (£ *worth*)

| | | Purchasing sectors i.e. Users of input | | | |
| | | Businesses | | Households | |
| | | Agri-culture | Cloth-ing | (Consump-tion) | (Gross outputs) |
|---|---|---|---|---|---|
| Supplying sectors i.e. sources of output | Businesses: | | | | |
| | Agriculture | — | 15 | 10 | (25) |
| | Clothing | 5 | — | 85 | (90) |
| | Households (Labour) | 20 | 75 | | |
| | (Gross inputs) | (25) | (90) | | |

thought of as consisting partly of boots, which are items of equipment for farm workers. If we now add a few numbers to indicate the precise amounts of inputs and outputs involved during a given period of time, we can represent the working of the economy in Table 2.1.

Each of the three sectors of the economy is shown twice in the table, once in its role as producer and once as consumer. The pro-

3. The table is prepared on the assumptions that

| Produces | Sells to | | | Uses inputs of | | |
| | Clothing | Agricul-ture | House-holds | Labour | Clothing | Agric. products |
|---|---|---|---|---|---|---|
| Agriculture 25 | 15 | — | 10 | 20 | 5 | — |
| Clothing 90 | — | 5 | 85 | 75 | — | 15 |

ducing, or supplying, sectors appear as rows; the purchasing, or using, sectors as columns. Reading across the top row, we find that the agricultural sector supplied £15 of product (the wool it needed) to the clothing industry, and it sold the remainder of its output, £10, direct to households. Its total gross output was therefore £25. The clothing industry, on the other hand, sold £5 worth of boots to agriculture, and £85 of clothing to households, making a total gross output of £90.

If we now read down the table we can obtain some of the same information, but from the user's point of view; e.g. the agricultural industry used £5 worth of input from the clothing industry. Total agricultural inputs (production costs) therefore add up to £25—£20 worth of labour and £5 worth of clothing. The clothing industry, on the other hand, used £15 worth of input from agriculture and £75 worth of labour, making a total input cost of £90.

The purpose of drawing up input–output tables of this kind for an economy is to enable an attempt to be made to work out the final effects of any given change of output by one or more industries. Suppose the clothing industry were to expand. It would need addi-

Table 2.2   **Total requirements per £100 of final industrial output in terms of net**

|  | Agri-culture 1 | Forestry and fishing 2 | Coal mining 3 | Other mining and quarry-ing 4 | Food 5 | Drink and tobacco 6 | Mineral oil refining 7 |
|---|---|---|---|---|---|---|---|
| 1 Agriculture | 58·4 | 0·1 | — | — | 12·2 | 2·0 | 0·1 |
| 2 Forestry and fishing | 0·1 | 67·3 | 0·4 | — | 0·4 | — | — |
| 3 Coal mining | 1·2 | 0·3 | 72·4 | 1·6 | 1·5 | 1·0 | 1·0 |
| 4 Other mining and quarrying | 0·1 | — | 0·1 | 44·4 | 0·2 | 0·1 | 0·2 |
| 5 Food | 5·4 | — | — | 0·1 | 32·0 | 0·9 | 0·1 |
| 6 Drink and tobacco | 0·2 | — | — | — | 0·2 | 49·5 | — |
| 7 Mineral oil refining | 0·2 | 0·5 | 0·1 | 0·1 | 0·1 | 0·1 | 10·8 |
| 8 Other chemicals, etc. | 3·9 | 0·5 | 0·9 | 3·5 | 3·4 | 1·0 | 4·0 |
| 9 Metal manufacture | 0·5 | 0·6 | 2·9 | 1·3 | 0·7 | 0·6 | 0·3 |
| 10 Shipbuilding | — | 3·8 | — | — | 0·1 | — | 0·3 |
| 11 Motor vehicles | 0·2 | 0·1 | 0·1 | 0·8 | 0·2 | 0·3 | 0·1 |
| 12 Aircraft | — | — | — | — | — | — | 0·1 |
| 13 Other vehicles | 0·1 | — | — | 0·1 | 0·1 | 0·1 | — |
| 14 Other engineering | 2·1 | 1·1 | 3·3 | 5·5 | 2·8 | 2·5 | 0·9 |
| 15 Textiles | 0·3 | 4·0 | 0·6 | 0·2 | 0·5 | 0·2 | 0·1 |
| 16 Leather and clothing | 0·1 | — | 0·1 | — | 0·1 | — | — |
| 17 Other manufacturing | 3·0 | 0·9 | 3·5 | 3·5 | 3·5 | 3·7 | 1·9 |

Source: *Economic Trends*, No. 178, August 1968, (H.M.S.O.).

tional agricultural production. But, expansion of agriculture would, in its turn, call for more clothing. And more clothing would call for even more agriculture, and so on. Now, if we know exactly what are the requirements that one industry, for a given expansion, has for the products of other industries we can use the input–output table to calculate the final size of each industry for the given expansion of one of them, after all inter-industry repercussions have been allowed for. In our example, we are, in fact, assuming that every increase in clothing production by £1 requires one sixth of £1 worth of agricultural output (£15 out of £90). Similarly, each increase in agricultural production by £1 requires one-fifth of £1 worth of clothing output (£5 out of £25). These fractions are called the **input coefficients**.

To be of practical value, an input–output table must distinguish between more than two sectors, and input coefficients must be reliable. An input–output table for the year 1963 published by the U.K. government in 1968 used nearly thirty sectors. Table 2.2 shows the input coefficients for the U.K. which have been calculated from it. For the sake of simplicity only a portion of the table has been re-

output, 1963

| Other chemicals, etc. 8 | Metal manufacture 9 | Ship building 10 | Motor vehicles 11 | Air-craft 12 | Other vehicles 13 | Other engineering 14 | Textiles 15 | Leather and clothing 16 | Other manufacturing 17 |
|---|---|---|---|---|---|---|---|---|---|
| 0·3 | — | — | 0·1 | — | — | — | 1·4 | 0·4 | 0·1 |
| 0·1 | 0·1 | — | — | — | — | — | — | — | 0·1 |
| 7·2 | 1·8 | 0·9 | 1·4 | 0·8 | 1·4 | 1·1 | 1·4 | 1·0 | 2·2 |
| 0·3 | 0·7 | 0·2 | 0·3 | 0·1 | 0·2 | 0·3 | — | 0·1 | 0·9 |
| 0·6 | 0·1 | — | 0·1 | — | — | 0·1 | 0·2 | 0·1 | 0·1 |
| 0·1 | — | — | — | — | — | — | — | — | 0·1 |
| 0·5 | 0·2 | 0·1 | 0·1 | 0·1 | 0·2 | 0·1 | 0·1 | 0·1 | 0·1 |
| 39·7 | 3·0 | 1·4 | 2·5 | 0·9 | 1·3 | 1·7 | 1·0 | 1·1 | 2·3 |
| 1·5 | 44·5 | 6·1 | 8·7 | 4·0 | 8·4 | 7·2 | 0·3 | 0·6 | 0·9 |
| — | — | 51·1 | — | — | — | — | — | — | — |
| 0·2 | 0·2 | 0·1 | 32·3 | 1·0 | 0·2 | 0·4 | 0·1 | 0·2 | 0·3 |
| — | — | — | — | 57·5 | — | — | — | — | — |
| 0·1 | 0·3 | 0·1 | 0·2 | 0·2 | 48·4 | 0·2 | — | — | 0·1 |
| 3·5 | 4·7 | 9·4 | 13·4 | 6·8 | 6·7 | 54·4 | 1·3 | 2·8 | 2·9 |
| 0·5 | 0·2 | 0·4 | 0·9 | 0·4 | 0·5 | 0·5 | 55·7 | 14·5 | 1·7 |
| 0·1 | — | 0·2 | 0·3 | 0·1 | — | 0·1 | 0·1 | 41·8 | 0·1 |
| 3·7 | 2·0 | 3·1 | 6·8 | 2·3 | 3·6 | 3·8 | 0·8 | 3·4 | 51·2 |

produced here, but it is enough to demonstrate dramatically the degree of interdependence which exists in the British economy, and some of the specialisation which takes place.

To find from Table 2.2 the input requirements for output expansion of £100 in any industry, simply read down the column for that sector. For example, £100 of extra output by the motor vehicle industry is seen to require 10p (£0·10) of extra output from agriculture; no more forestry and fishing; £1·4 extra output from the coal industry; and so on, including even an additional £32·3 worth of its own product. You need motor vehicles to make motor vehicles.

It would be dangerous to leave this subject without pointing out that exercises with input–output tables must be interpreted with caution—especially when they are used for predicting the consequences of *future* changes. Being based, inevitably, upon *past* history, they cannot be relied on always to be applicable to the future in a world where many things, including production techniques, are liable to change. The construction of input–output tables does, however, give something of a feeling for the job of the economist, seeking patterns of consistent behaviour in the relationships between different sectors of the economy in the process of production.

# Chapter 3

# Markets and Prices

In the previous two chapters we drew attention to some of the forces which influence decisions about consumption and production, and emphasised that the economist is constantly on the lookout for consistent patterns of behaviour of households and businesses. We must now consider more closely the ways in which production and consumption decisions affect each other. But, before we get to grips with this matter, there is one crucial point that must be made. Indeed, it is central to the nature of economics, and the majority of introductory textbooks deal with it in the very first pages.

## Scarcity and economic goods

So far, we have identified a number of characteristics of goods and services which affect economic decision-taking, but we have not yet dealt with one fundamental property that a good must possess before an economist will pay attention to it. This is the quality of **scarcity**.

An economist might be interested, for example, in how much petrol is sucked into a car's engine, but not in how much air is drawn in with it. He might want to know how much people enjoy a swim in the local pool, but not how much they enjoy a dip in the sea. Why? The oxygen in the air is quite as important to the working of a motor car engine as is petrol. And the most obvious differences between swimming pools and the sea are things like salt content, chlorine and waves, which do not sound like critical economic matters.

The explanation is simple enough. Petrol and swimming pools have a prime characteristic in common which distinguishes them from air and sea water, and which is in no way related to their physical properties. It is this. Petrol and swimming pools are not available in sufficient quantities to enable people to have all that they want of them. In other words, they are not abundant, like air and sea water, but are, in contrast, 'scarce', and it is necessary to make a **choice** of how much of each of them is to be produced.

Economists are interested only in the production and consumption of goods and services which are scarce or, more precisely, of goods and services which are produced by factors of production which are themselves scarce. The reason why it is the scarcity of factors, rather than of goods, that is basically important is that there would be little difficulty in producing enough of any one good for everybody to have as much of it as he wanted. Although stereograms are scarce enough, there would really be no great difficulty in providing every family in Britain with half a dozen of them. And although lemonade is scarce and water is not, the economy could produce enough pop to supply all the drinking needs of the nation if this is what was really wanted.

**Opportunity cost**

There is, naturally, a catch to all this. If we gave everyone, say, six stereograms, or enough lemonade to shave in, we would have to do without something else that we value. To make stereograms, labour, machinery, wood, and other raw materials are necessary; but these factors of production are also required for the manufacture of almost all the other goods and services that societies want. That is to say, the factors themselves are scarce. We do not have enough labour or capital to make as much of everything which we want at the same time. If we use our factors to make a stereogram, we sacrifice the chance to use them for another purpose. There is a real cost involved in employing any scarce factors of production for a particular use. Economists call this **opportunity cost**, to stress the fundamental lost opportunity which occurs when a production decision involving a scarce factor is made. This concept is central to economics.

*Relative scarcity*

Economic goods, then, are defined as those which are produced by at least one scarce factor of production, but the scarcity of the factor is not absolute. It is relative to the value which people place upon it. In the case of water, for example, there is so much more of it falling as rain in Britain than people want that it is an international joke. But in India, and in California, water is by no means abundant and, even in Britain, water is not freely available in ample quantities to every home. Scarce factors of production are needed to make provision of adequate supplies for domestic purposes.

Moreover, even petrol need not necessarily be scarce in the true economic sense of scarce relative to demand. If, for example, petrol was proved to emit certain ultrasonic rays which caused fatal heart disease, with the result that the demand for it dropped to zero, petrol would no longer be a scarce good to economists. If, however, there were merely a shift in people's tastes away from the things (such as motoring and oil heating) for which petrol is used, it would become relatively less, but still to some extent, scarce.

## The gap between wants and resources

Another way of approaching the idea of relative scarcity is to realise that there is a gap between the wants which people have and the resources which are available for their satisfaction. We can develop this idea and obtain some important conclusions by considering a simplified model economy, where decisions are to be taken on what to produce over the coming period of time, say, a year. In our economy, we include several factors of production, but only two goods which are produced by them. The nature of the goods is irrelevant. To think of an economy subsisting on only two products is so clearly unreasonable that there is no point in pretending that they are realistic. Let us call them, therefore, spaghetti and overcoats.

Imagine, then, that all resources are used to produce either

Table 3.1 **Possible output combinations per week**

| Combination | Overcoats | Spaghetti |
|---|---|---|
| A | 1,000 | 0 |
| B | 750 | 125 |
| C | 500 | 250 |
| D | 250 | 375 |
| E | 0 | 500 |

spaghetti or overcoats, or a combination of the two. Consider, further, that we know how much of these goods could be produced per year if resources were employed as efficiently as possible. Say that 1,000 overcoats could be produced if there was no need for spaghetti; 500 (tons of) spaghetti if no one wanted overcoats; or that any of the following combinations of the two goods could be produced—750 overcoats and 125 spaghetti; 500 overcoats and 250 spaghetti; or 250 overcoats and 375 spaghetti.

All these production (or output) possibilities can be set out in the form of a table known as a production possibility schedule (Table 3.1).

Output possibilities can also be represented graphically. If we measure overcoats on the vertical axis and spaghetti on the horizontal, we can plot each point on the graph (Figure 3.1).

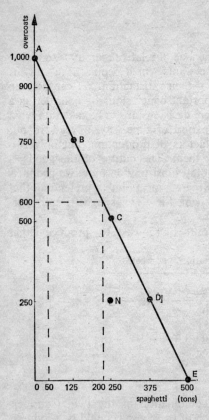

Figure 3.1 A production possibility curve, exhibiting constant opportunity costs

In Figure 3.1 point *A* shows output when all resources are devoted to overcoats (1,000). Point *E* shows that 500 spaghetti can be produced when no resources are used for overcoat production. Point *C* shows the maximum possible output if resources are divided equally between the two goods, so that 500 overcoats and 250 spaghetti are available, and so on. This diagram emphasises the fact that the real opportunity cost of producing more of one good is the reduction in output of the other. If we join together points $A$ to $E$ and assume that all intermediate positions along $AE$ represent combinations of spaghetti and overcoats which can be produced (e.g. 50 spaghetti and 900 overcoats; 200 spaghetti and 600 overcoats, etc.) we have, in fact, a line which represents all the production possibilities which are open to society. This line is called a **production possibility curve**, a **transformation curve**, or sometimes a **production frontier**. It has certain features to which we must draw attention.

i. It represents only the maximum combinations of the two goods which could be produced, if resources are all fully employed and organised as efficiently as possible. Any combination of goods within the space between the line $AE$ and the origin $O$ is possible, but all would involve some waste of resources. At $N$, for example, 250 overcoats and 250 spaghetti would be produced. This must be an inefficient use of resources, or indicate that some are simply lying idle, since we know that if only 250 overcoats were produced, there would be enough resources to produce, not 250 tons of spaghetti, but 375. Alternatively, if only 250 spaghetti were produced, there would be enough resources left for 500 overcoats. In other words $C$ or $D$ are better combinations of output than $N$.

ii. The slope of the curve is a measure of the opportunity cost of producing more of one good. The figures in Table 3.1 tell us, in numerical terms, what the opportunity cost is. We can describe this cost in either of two ways. If we adopt the viewpoint of using resources for spaghetti production rather than for overcoats, the opportunity cost of 500 spaghetti is 1,000 overcoats; or, on average, the cost of 1 ton of spaghetti is 2 overcoats. Alternatively, if we look at the cost of overcoat production *in terms of spaghetti given up*, 1,000 overcoats 'cost' 500 spaghetti; or, on average 1 overcoat means the loss of $\frac{1}{2}$ ton of spaghetti.

Now that we know the numerical value of the opportunity cost let us return to the diagram and find its graphical expression. Imagine all resources are used in overcoat production, i.e. the economy is at point $A$ in Figure 3.2. Suppose, now, it is decided, to produce 50 spaghetti, represented by point $B$ in Figure 3.2, where the production possibility curve $AE$ is reproduced. The cost of doing so is the reduction in overcoat production implied in the move, which we know to be 100 overcoats. Or, again, on average, the cost of each ton of spaghetti is 2 overcoats. Moreover, as we proceed down the production possibility curve, using all our resources with maximum efficiency, we shall always have the same opportunity cost facing us— 1 ton more spaghetti always costs 2 overcoats.

The reason why the slope of the line describes the opportunity cost should now be clear. It may be further clarified in Figure 3.3, where a second production possibility curve, *AF*, has been added. On the new curve, we assume that the economy is able to produce the same number of overcoats as before, but only half as many tons of spaghetti. If now we again contemplate moving resources from 100 overcoats to spaghetti production, we shall get, not 50 tons of spaghetti, but only 25. That is to say, the opportunity cost of 25 spaghetti is now 100 overcoats. If we still really want 50 spaghetti, we shall have to give up 200 overcoats—i.e. 1 spaghetti costs 4 overcoats on the average, and the line *AF* is twice as steep as *AE*.

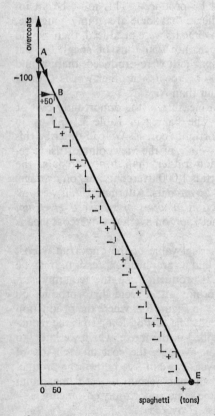

*Figure 3.2* Production possibility curve, where 1 ton of sphagetti has constant opportunity costs of 2 overcoats

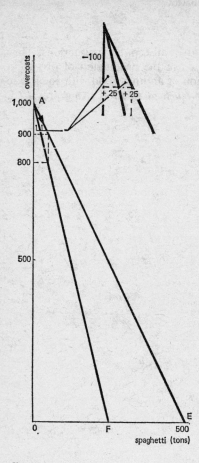

*Figure 3.3* Production possibility curves, *AE* and *AF*. The latter exhibits higher opportunity costs of spaghetti in terms of overcoats

## Constant costs

In the examples used so far, the cost of spaghetti in terms of overcoats is not affected by the amount of either good being produced. In other words, we have been assuming what are called **constant costs**. This was illustrated geometrically in Figures 3.1, 3.2, and 3.3 by the fact that the production possibility curves are straight lines. The cost of producing one more of either good in terms of the other does not change as we move along *AE*, or along *AF*. There is a proportional relationship between them.

## Increasing costs

But, constant costs are not found in all economic situations. They imply that the resources employed in the production of one good can be combined in the production of another good with equal ease and efficiency, *regardless of how much of either* is being produced.

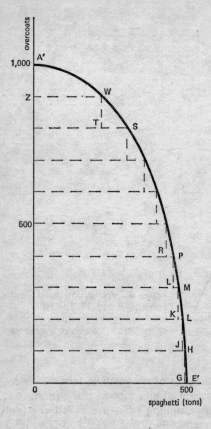

Figure 3.4 Production possibility curve exhibiting increasing opportunity cost

Such a situation occurs if all resources are, as we shall see, neutral as between differing uses. But this is not very likely. One reason is that although the two goods can be made by exactly the same resources (labour and land, for example), each factor of production is probably not equally efficient at producing spaghetti *and* overcoats. Men work in both lines of output, but their skills are not the same in each. So when resources have to be transferred from, say, spaghetti to overcoat production, it is natural to expect that the men first released will be those who are least skilled at spaghetti production. Then, as more and more resources are moved over, it becomes increasingly necessary to transfer the efficient spaghetti workers to overcoat production. The cost of producing an additional overcoat tends to rise, involving the loss of more and more spaghetti. The further the economy moves north-west along $E'A'$ in Figure 3.4, the more the cost of overcoats, in terms of spaghetti, increases.

This may be seen quite easily from the graph, where $OA'$ has been divided into equal units ($GJ = JK = KM = WT = ZA$, etc.) Start at $E'$, with all resources in spaghetti production, and move towards $A'$ in 'jumps' representing equal increases in overcoat production. The cost of doing so, in terms of foregone spaghetti, rises all the time, from $E'G$ to $HJ$ to $LK$, etc., until eventually it reaches $ST$ and $WZ$, as the last units of resources leave the industry and the spaghetti mills close down.

Another reason for expecting cost to increase as resources move from one output to another, has nothing to do with acquired or innate differential skills of the labour force or of any other factor of production. It is concerned with the *proportions* in which factors of production are combined with each other. To demonstrate this, let us assume that some combinations of factors are better than others; that spaghetti, for instance, can be produced most efficiently with a relatively large amount of land, while overcoat production is cheaper with relatively large numbers of workers.

Consider again what happens as we move from $E'$ up towards $A'$, increasing overcoat production. At first, all resources are producing spaghetti, and the first factors released are likely to be largely labour since these are relatively abundant in spaghetti production. All to the good, of course, for the overcoat producers. A lot of labour is what they need, not a lot of land. Worse, however, is to follow as more overcoat production is wanted, and we move further up $E'A'$. Precisely because a relatively large amount of labour was released to start with, there is less available now. Instead, as the transfer of resources continues to the end, relatively larger and larger amounts of land inevitably become available. Lowering output of spaghetti means, therefore, that fewer and fewer overcoats can be made with the newly acquired factors. Certainly, total overcoat production rises, but the opportunity cost of one extra overcoat, in terms of spaghetti given up, also rises.

We shall return to this question again in Chapter 5, where the idea of *diminishing returns* to a factor of production will be more fully explained. We may be satisfied now with the realisation that a production possibility curve which represents rising real opportunity costs of each good in terms of the other as production increases, is not uncommon. We recognise its shape as a true curve, convex to the origin, as in Figure 3.4.

## The meaning of choice

One basic aspect of the argument about scarcity and the related notion of opportunity cost, is that so long as there is a shortage of goods and services relative to the demand for them, there must inevitably be problems of choice. The household must choose how to spend its limited income, and the business must choose what factors of production it should buy. Economics is essentially concerned with such problems of choice. Indeed, the subject has even been dubbed the 'science of choice'. When people talk of the existence of the **economic problem**, they are referring to the way in which an economy, or a person, chooses to allocate scarce resources among all the competing uses to which they may be put.

Economic problems exist both for the individual and for society as a whole. In each case the notion of scarcity must be regarded in the relative sense to which attention was drawn earlier. Table 1.2 in Chapter 1 (page 11), for example, demonstrates that the gap between resources and needs is not the same for households in different income classes. For those with incomes of less than £6 a week in 1969, there could hardly have been enough of any goods and services to satisfy quite low requirements. But even those households with £60 or more coming in per week are faced with the problem of choice. If an extra £1 is available next week, what will they do with it? More clothing would 'cost' less entertainment, or fewer other goods, and it is a *real* cost so long as the household does not have a large enough income to buy as much of everything as it wishes, and to save as much as it wants for the future.

## The affluent society

Present day Britain is sometimes called an affluent society. The United States even more frequently so, because income per head is significantly higher there. Does this mean that the economic problem has begun to disappear?

Certainly rising incomes have made many problems of choice less urgent than they were a hundred years ago, or than they are today in countries like India and China, where millions of people may not have enough food. But, although there are a handful of multimillion-aires who have so much that they cannot be thought of as facing any personal economic problems, for any nation as a whole and for the vast majority of people in it, the economic problem still exists though in a perhaps less urgent, modern form. Although teenage factory workers with relatively high incomes may sometimes seem to have nearly everything they want, they would nearly always also like some of the things that the rich possess—faster cars, for example. Moreover, the range of choice a person allows himself is itself set by his limited means. A man only starts to think of owning an Aston Martin, for example, if his income is high enough to make it a real possibility.

## Leisure as a scarce commodity

We must not forget that every one, even a millionaire, is faced with the economic problem of how best to spend the twenty-four hours of the day. Ignoring, for the sake of simplicity, man's need for

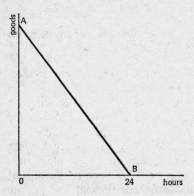

*Figure 3.5* The opportunity cost of goods in terms of leisure sacrificed

sleep, the choice can be portrayed as fundamentally one between work and leisure. In so far as work results in output, the cost of more goods and services is the leisure that has to be given up in order to produce them. Figure 3.5 illustrates the alternatives available: twenty-four hours of leisure and no goods, *OA* goods and no leisure, and all the combinations of leisure and goods implied by the line *AB* (which is drawn as a straight one, implying that one hour's more work always brings a reward of the same number of goods). If, more realistically, there were diminishing returns to work, the line would be convex to the origin, like $A'E'$ in Figure 3.4 (page 40).

## Social versus private wants

The existence of scarcity in an affluent society is also demonstrated by what are known as public goods. These are things like roads, prisons, and welfare services, which (for reasons to be considered in a later chapter) are often provided by the state. They are said to satisfy social as distinguished from private wants, which an individual

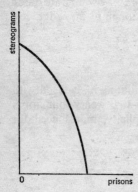

*Figure 3.6* The opportunity cost of private goods in terms of public goods

satisfies for himself by buying food, clothing, etc., in the market place.

Opinions differ as to what goods and services should be supplied by the government, and what the individual should be left to buy for himself. An American economist, John K. Galbraith described the reasons why he thought that the U.S. economy was underproviding for social wants, such as schools, at the expense of private wants, such as automobiles.[1] Galbraith's argument has been criticised, but there is no room for doubt about the fact that social and private wants compete. The more resources are used to make cars and stereograms, the less they are available for state education, the national health service, and defence. Figure 3.6 illustrates the choice between a typical private good (stereograms) and a public good (prisons).

1. J. K. Galbraith, *The Affluent Society* (Penguin Books, 1962).

## Economic growth

A production possibility curve for an economy is drawn to represent the nature of a particular set of choices during a given period of time, such as a year. It reflects the underlying state of technology at that time, as well as the available resources. Any change in either matter would result in a shift of the production possibility curve itself.

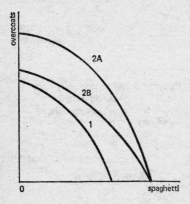

Figure 3.7 An increase in productivity shifts the production possibility curve to the right

In Figure 3.7, the original situation of Figure 3.4 (page 40) is repeated in curve 1. Curves 2A and 2B, on the other hand, represent situations in a later year, when it becomes possible to produce more of both goods than before, because of improved technology, population growth, the acquisition of new natural resources, or some other change. The difference between 2A and 2B is that, in the former, the increased productivity is *proportionately the same* in both spaghetti and overcoats. 2B on the other hand implies that the change increased the supply of those factors of production which are relatively more important in spaghetti than in overcoat production.

Outward shifting of a production possibility curve might be due to the fact that in some previous year the economy decided to devote resources to building up its stock of capital goods. This, we know, must have had a real cost in terms of fewer consumption goods in the earlier period. (See Figure 3.8.) Here, however, the nature of the opportunity cost must be interpreted with a little more care. In so far as the additional capital shifts the production possibility curve to the north-west, away from the origin, the cost of foregone consumption at the time the capital is being built up is, partly at least, offset by the extra consumer goods that can later be made available. Indeed, one of the most important problems of choice facing an economy concerns the rate at which it is prepared to forego present consumption in order to have more to consume in the future. As we shall learn later, holding down consumption to increase invest-

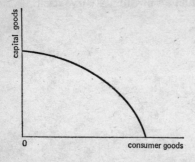

*Figure 3.8* The opportunity cost of capital goods is the consumer goods that must temporarily be sacrificed

ment is one of the prime determinants of the rate of growth that an economy can enjoy.

## Prices and markets

The first part of this chapter has been confined to describing the problems that scarcity of resources, relative to wants, raise in an economy. The last lap in our introductory overview is concerned with the ways in which the kind of society we live in solves these problems. We have seen several examples of choices that face individuals and nations. But, in fact, it is possible to reduce them to a number of basic types, of which two are of outstanding importance:

    i. **What** goods and services shall be produced?
    ii. **How** are they to be produced?

Consider the first of these problems. The question what shall be produced must be interpreted as meaning how much of each of the different goods and services will society decide to use its scarce resources for? How many overcoats, stereograms, schools, prisons? How much spaghetti, clothing, Christmas pudding, and starch? The list is enormous, for it should include everything that society is capable of producing with any resources which are in limited supply.

## Traditional societies

It must be admitted at once that there is no single answer to the question of how a society should solve the problem of how to allocate its scarce resources. In a self-sufficient society, the decision of what to produce may be made by tradition. A man hunts because his father hunted before him. A girl cooks because that is what her mother did. Each family or tribal unit is virtually self-sufficient, and that is an end to it.

In more modern industrialised or semi-industrialised economies, tradition may still have a role in the making of production decisions. But the specialisation of modern production methods demands that more complex techniques be employed. Families are no longer self-sufficient, and some form of exchange—whereby welders, for example, can buy the output of farm workers—is needed. Modern societies have evolved a highly specialised institution to perform this function. It is through the medium of **money** that factors can receive rewards for their services, and buy such goods and services as they happen to want. We discuss this in Chapter 5, pp. 85–6.

## Command economies

There are two basically different ways in which complex modern economies can take their decisions on what to produce. In the first, a central agency may simply decide, for everyone, how the scarce resources at the disposal of the country should be allocated between the various competing uses. As far as economies are concerned, it does not matter whether the agency is democratically elected, a benevolent dictatorship, or even a tyrannical despot. As long as the decision on what to produce is taken *centrally*, the economy is known as **command**, and we can ignore the political pros and cons.

## Market economies

Britain is not a command economy at the present time, although it came very close to being one during both the First and Second World Wars. Even in peacetime, however, the government decides how much to spend on public goods for the satisfaction of social wants such as defence, and a large part of health and education. But the bulk of decisions about what to produce in Britain are not taken directly by the government at all. As we know from Chapters 1 and 2, decisions about the production of private goods are taken by the business sector of the economy, though they are also influenced by the decisions which individuals wish to take as consumers of goods and services.

For the private sector of the economy, where stereograms and overcoats are produced, there is no central government agency controlling production. Instead, a form of social institution has evolved which allows producers and consumers to get in touch with one another. This institution is simply a **market**, and the communication that buyers and sellers have with each other is a monetary one, through the medium of what is known as the **price-mechanism**.

## The price mechanism

A market in economics is, therefore, no more than a place or organisation whereby producers, or sellers of a good, can get in touch with those who may want to buy what they are offering for sale. Goods are not, however, given away but are bought and sold, and it is possible to regard the movements in their prices as acting as *signalling* devices which indicate whether too much or too little of each good or service is being produced.

Consider, for example, the market for a single commodity, say tomatoes, during a given period of time, say a week. On one side of the market there are the potential tomato consumers; on the other side are the sellers of tomatoes.

Suppose that the sellers offer their stock for sale at a price which, if they sell it all, will cover their costs plus a modest profit. At this price, however, it does not follow that the quantity that consumers wish to buy will necessarily be exactly the right amount to clear the market. If it is not, then the price must be either too high or too low. If it is too high there will be an excess of **supply** over **demand**. And, if all producers are to dispose of their tomatoes before they perish, some of them will have to lower the price. And once price has fallen in one part of the market, it is difficult for any single producer to charge a higher one. Competition among sellers tends to bring the price down for all.

On the other hand, price may be too low, in the sense that households wish to buy more at this ruling price than sellers are prepared to sell. In other words, there is an excess of demand over supply. The effect in this case is the exact opposite of that described in the previous paragraph. Now it is the buyers who are in competition with each other. There are not enough tomatoes for everyone who wants to buy them. Some sellers will soon catch on and find that they can sell their stocks even if they raise the price. As before, once price has risen in a part of the market, other sellers may soon follow suit. Competition among consumers for a limited quantity tends to raise market price.

There is, therefore, a tendency for price to move up and down in the market to bring about an equality between the quantity of tomatoes that sellers want to sell and that which consumers wish to purchase. In other words, the price mechanism tends to equate supply and demand. When the wishes of sellers and purchasers in the market happen to be the same then price is said to be at an **equilibrium** level. Supply and demand are equal.

## The market in disequilibrium

It is instructive to observe how the price mechanism works in disequilibrium—i.e., when the market has been in equilibrium, and some external change disturbs it. The argument is not basically affected by whether the initial change comes from the demand side or from the supply side, as for example when costs of production alter after a new machine is invented. Let us, however, examine the effects of a change which originates on the demand side.

We know from our brief look at household expenditure patterns in Chapter I that demand is likely to be influenced by several factors such as income, tastes and family size. Let us suppose that the size of families among consumers increases. How would this affect the price of tomatoes, and the quantity bought and sold? Figure 1.1 on page 15 suggests that the proportion of income spent on food rises with size of family. So let us assume that the rise in average family size implies also an increase in the demand for tomatoes, in the sense that households wish to purchase larger quantities at each and every price, including that which until now has been the equilibrium price in the market. In these circumstances, there is an excess of demand over supply, and this tends to produce a rise in price, which acts as a signal to both sellers and buyers. The higher price will tend to choke off some of the new demand, for only those who value tomatoes highly will be prepared to pay more for them, and price will settle at a new, higher, equilibrium.

The rise in price may have a second effect, however. Provided that there has been no change in the production costs of tomatoes, we would expect that sellers would increase the quantity they wish to sell. If they were making a profit before, they would make a larger one with a higher price, and thus other producers—of cucumbers, for example—might be tempted to switch production to tomatoes. So in the end, when the market has finally settled at a new equilibrium, we may find that the increase in demand, working through changing price, has brought about an increase in supply to meet it.

## The operation of market forces

Such is the way in which market forces are said to work. The simplicity and low cost of administration of the price mechanism can be very appealing. Indeed Adam Smith wrote of it as the 'invisible hand' which guides resources into their best uses, as indicated by preferences of consumers for different products, relative to costs of production. Moreover, the wishes of consumers and producers are harmonised through the price mechanism *in spite of*, or rather *because of*, the fact that each individual in the market is doing his best to look after his own interest.

This is, perhaps, most obvious on the demand side. If the price of a good changes, people will tend to buy different quantities of it, because its opportunity cost relative to other goods has altered. By allocating expenditure differently from before, consumers are most likely to get the maximum satisfaction out of their total income.

Less obvious may be the fact that the independent attempt by each producer to maximise his profits can also be in the interest of consumers. If demand increases, and price rises in consequence, the incentive of higher profits may be what brings forth a matching increase in supply. Little wonder that some nineteenth-century philosophers studying these matters were enthusiastic supporters of a freely working price mechanism for equating the wishes of self-seeking producers and consumers. They could see that prices act as signals on a track between buyers and sellers—*rationing* a limited supply among those prepared to pay most for it, and stimulating changes in supply in the light of changing conditions. The so-called **laissez-faire** philosophy of non-interference by the government in the working of the economy flourished on this kind of argument.

A formal treatment of the working of the price mechanism will be given in the next two chapters. But we must note in passing that efficient resource allocation as a result of changing prices depends upon a number of assumptions that must be made explicitly, and on the existence of certain preconditions. In so far as any of these are not present, the pricing system may be found lacking.

We shall return in the last but one chapter of this book to consider these matters more fully. Meanwhile we shall simply set out the main assumptions which must be made for the price mechanism to work efficiently. They are:

i. Buyers and sellers can, and do, maximise satisfaction and profits. Consumers know what they want and are prepared to back their desires with hard cash. Producers know which goods are the most profitable to produce, and they act on this knowledge. There must be no public goods (like defence) which are consumed collectively by the community at large, and which are characterised as those on which people *as individuals* do not want to spend their money.

ii. There is effective competition on both sides of the market which, as we have seen, leads to price changes whenever changes in the conditions of supply or demand occur, as when tastes change, or new production techniques are discovered.

iii. Supply and demand are responsive to changes in price—at high prices supply exceeds demand, and at low prices demand exceeds supply. In other words, consumers wish to buy more of a good as price falls, and sellers wish to offer more for sale as price rises.

iv. Supply and demand respond reasonably quickly to price changes. Many complicated factors lie behind this assumption. We may note, in particular, the fact that supply adjustments are made more speedily when factors of production can move easily between firms making different products.

v. The distribution of income and wealth between persons is in some sense satisfactory, or 'optimal'. The importance of this assumption can be understood if the pricing system is seen as reflecting consumer wants as expressed in the prices that people are prepared to pay for different goods and services. The price mechanism is rather like an electoral system with money for votes. Consumers 'vote' for products by spending their money on those goods that please them. Unlike the way in which members of parliament are elected, however, the number of 'votes' held by each individual is not the same, but is determined by his annual income and accumulated wealth. This is not to say that the actual distribution of money 'votes' that people possess is or is not regarded as acceptable. But we must assume that the distribution of income and wealth is ideal if we are to accept the proposition that the distribution of resources through the working of the price mechanism truly reflects the best wishes of the consumer.

vi. The institutional framework within which the pricing system operates is satisfactory. This requires there to be efficient markets for all goods and services, although it does not necessarily imply the existence of physical buildings or street markets. So long as buyers and sellers are in touch with each other a market exists, even if it is intangible because business is conducted by telephone. Additionally, there are other social institutions to be considered. Money, private property, and book-keeping are examples of institutions without which a pricing system would work quite differently, or might not even work at all. Such institutions affect the manner in which producers respond to market forces. So, too, does the framework of customs, rules and laws, which are generally needed if a market is to operate at all effectively. We should not overlook, also, the effect which many institutions, such as marriage and the family, have on the patterns of consumer expenditure. Supply and demand operate in a social setting, not in a vacuum.

### Factor, money and international markets

So far, the description of the mechanism by which price acts in the market place has been almost wholly concerned with the question of *what* goods the economy should use its limited resources to produce. There are, however, several kinds of market other than that for goods, and economists are interested in all of them. Many common features and principles exist in these different markets. In what economists call the *factor market*, for example, the forces of supply and demand operate as in the goods market, but here they act on the prices of factors of production—wages, interest, rent, and profits. They help to show how the price mechanism answers the question of *how* to produce a given output. Clearly, the best combination in which to employ factors of production depends upon their relative prices.

In the factor market we must also consider a third related economic problem—*who* shall consume the output that has been produced. Naturally, a man's income derived from his services as a factor will affect his power to buy goods and services; and the way in which he decides to distribute a given expenditure over the range of available products is relevant to the question of resource allocation between different goods. Matters like tastes and other determinants of household expenditure, which were mentioned in Chapter 1, enter the picture. There is, indeed, an overlap between the factor and goods markets, and economists have to consider them both at the same time.

Finally, we may mention two other major kinds of market which possess significantly different characteristics. One is the money market, where the lending and borrowing of money occurs, and financial assets are bought and sold. The other is the international market, where different national currencies circulate, and where individuals from different countries import and export goods and services and make other international transactions.

These four kinds of market—for goods, factors, money, and international transactions—provide the framework within which the price mechanism operates to answer not only the what? how? and who? questions that face an economy, but other subsidiary ones as well, such as *when* to consume? (now or later) and where to produce? (say, in Glasgow or in London). To see how they are answered we need a better understanding of the nature of supply and demand, and to this purpose we devote the next chapter.

Chapter 4

# Supply and Demand in the Market for Goods

---

### Introduction

In the last chapter we looked briefly at the way in which prices, acting as signals, direct production towards goods and services that people want to buy, and ration the available quantities among persons prepared to pay for them. Our present task is to examine more closely the working of supply, demand and price in the market place. In this chapter we will concentrate on the markets for goods or commodities. In the next, we will look at the working of the price mechanism in other kinds of market, such as those where factors of production are bought and sold.

We already know that the market price of a commodity depends upon demand and supply. Our next step is to examine more closely each of these. We shall proceed by considering demand and supply from the viewpoint of the individual consumer and supplier of goods. Then, by simply adding together demand by individuals, we can obtain what may be called total, or market, demand for a good. Similarly we can derive a notion of market supply, and finally put the two together to consider the formation of market price.

### Demand

The demand that is of interest to economists is that which is related to the quantities of a commodity that individuals would be prepared to purchase. This is not the same thing as the quantities that they 'need', or would like to have. Needs and wants obviously lie behind purchases; but resources are limited, and our concern is only with actual market behaviour as revealed in **effective demand** backed by willingness to spend money.

We know from the opening chapter that the amount of a commodity which people want to purchase is dependent upon many factors. Economists, however, find it convenient for expository purposes to concentrate upon one determinant at a time. The one in which prime interest resides is the price at which a commodity can be obtained.

Let us take an example of a specific good, ice cream, and let us assume that a person's demand for this good, per period of time, depends upon such forces as the price of ice cream, the price of chocolates, and other competing goods, the individual's income, his wealth, his tastes, the weather, and any other miscellaneous factors which may influence his desire to buy one. In the short run, we may reasonably suppose that all influences on demand, other than the price of an ice cream itself, do not change. We may then ignore the effect of all the other factors and concentrate on the demand for ice cream related only to its price.

This method of argument is commonly employed in economics, when behaviour is known to depend on several factors. In such circumstances the analysis may be very complicated, and economists simplify the problem by a process of abstraction—analysing the influence of each determinant in turn, on the assumption that other determining factors do not change. The assumption is known by the name *ceteris paribus*, from the latin 'other things remaining equal'. We shall use it several times in this book.[1]

To make the point clearer, we can imagine a list of the quantities of ice cream that would be bought at various prices. Such a list is called a **demand schedule**. Table 4.1 shows demand schedules for two

Table 4.1   (Hypothetical) Demand schedules for ice cream
*Quantities demanded per week*

| Price, pence | Alan | Bill | Bill and Alan |
|---|---|---|---|
| 8 | 1 | 0 | 1 |
| 7 | 2 | 0 | 2 |
| 6 | 3 | 2 | 5 |
| 5 | 4 | 4 | 8 |
| 4 | 5 | 6 | 11 |
| 3 | 6 | 8 | 14 |
| 2 | 7 | 10 | 17 |
| 1 | 8 | 12 | 20 |

individuals whom we call Alan and Bill. The example is, of course, hypothetical, but it serves to illustrate the fundamental idea that demand has no exact meaning by itself, but only in relation to a particular price.

Demand schedules like those in Table 4.1 can also be represented graphically. If we measure price on the vertical axis and quantity

1. The method is discussed in Chapter 9.

demanded on the horizontal, we can draw a diagram for Alan and another for Bill as in Figure 4.1 (i) and (ii). Each point on Alan's graph represents a particular price-quantity relationship: that is, the number of ice creams he would buy per week at a certain price. If we join up the points on the graph, we obtain what is known as Alan's **demand curve**, $D_A$, for ice cream. We do the same for Bill, whose demand curve is labelled $D_B$.

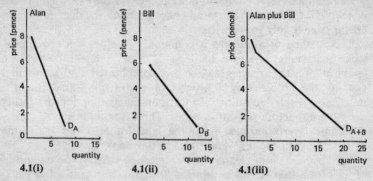

*Figure 4.1* Demand curves for individuals and the market demand for ice cream per week

If, now, we add together the demand schedules for Alan and Bill, and assume that they comprise the total number of persons who buy ice cream, we have in column three of Table 4.1 the total **market demand schedule**. Similarly, in Figure 4.1 (iii) we can 'add' the demand curves for the two persons. This is done by constructing the line $D_{A+B}$ in Figure 4.1 (iii), by adding horizontally the quantities demanded at each price. Thus at 8 pence and 7 pence each, only Alan buys ice cream, so the market demand curve is exactly the same as Alan's. At a price of 6 pence, however, Alan buys 3 ice creams, but Bill also buys 2, so the market demand is for 5 ice creams at that price, and so on.

All three demand curves are *downward sloping*. This feature is common to most demand curves. It reflects the fact that more of a good tends to be demanded the lower its price. One should not accept this as being necessarily true of all goods at all times. But it seems reasonable enough for the market demand curve to be downward sloping, since a fall in price can bring new consumers into the market.

Why, however, we may ask, should an individual's demand for a good be greater at low prices than at high ones? Again we cannot generalise for all commodities, all persons, and all times. But it seems sensible that the *extra* satisfaction, **or utility**, which one gets from *additional* amounts of a good tends to fall as one has more of it. Alan, in our example, would be prepared to pay 8 pence for a single ice cream a week, but would only buy 2 a week if the price were 7 pence, and it would take a price of 2 pence to induce him to buy 7 ice creams. We are probably safe in thinking that this is because he feels less extra satisfaction from two ice creams than from his first, and even less extra enjoyment from 7 rather than 6 ice creams per week. This characteristic of demand is known as the principle of **diminishing marginal utility**, because it implies that, although total utility increases with rising quantities, each (marginal) *increase* in consumption of a good gives less *extra* satisfaction (or utility) than previous units.

## *Income and substitution effects*

We may gain further insight into the reasons why demand curves tend to slope downwards by considering that there are really two distinct aspects of a price fall that lead to change in the quantity purchased. These are known as the **substitution effect** and the **income effect**. The nature of the substitution effect is obvious. When the price of any good falls while the prices of all other goods remain unchanged, there is a natural tendency for people to buy it instead of other goods—that is, to substitute it for similar or competing commodities. But there is an additional reason why demand may increase when price falls. For among our *ceteris paribus* assumptions, it may be recalled, is that of a constant level of the consumer's income. But when an individual has a fixed **money income** and the price of one of the goods he buys falls, this effectively means that his **real income** rises. Now, a rise in real income means that a person has more to spend on all goods. It is likely that he will use some of this extra to buy more of the commodity whose price has fallen.

We have already distinguished (see Chapter 1, page 13) between 'normal' and 'inferior' goods, referring to those whose consumption rises (or falls) when income rises (or falls) as 'normal', and those which are bought in smaller quantities as income rises as 'inferior'. Provided that the good whose price falls is not an inferior good, the income effect of the price change, as well as the substitution effect, will tend to increase the quantity demanded.

Although most demand curves, as argued above, slope downwards, the steepness of the slope varies from one commodity to another. To put the matter another way, when the price of a good changes, the extent to which this leads to a change in demand is not the same for all goods.

The reasons for this are related, to a considerable extent, to what we have called the substitution effect. The more and better substitutes that a good has, the more one may expect demand to increase for a fall in price (or to decrease for a rise in price). In part, this may merely reflect how closely a commodity is defined. 'Kodak 35 mm cameras' have more substitutes than '35 mm cameras', which in turn have more substitutes than 'cameras'. But it is also true that there are more good substitutes for, say, tomato sauce, than for, say, salt.

The income effect is also, of course, relevant to the extent to which demand for a good tends to respond to price changes. If the good is an inferior one, the income effect will dampen the substitution effect. For a normal good in contrast, the rise in real income tends to reinforce the increase in demand following a price fall. For any commodity, however, one can add that the more important the item in the consumer's budget, the stronger the income effect is likely to be. A good such as ice cream in our earlier example, obviously absorbs so small a part of a consumer's budget that a change in price of a few pence can hardly have a significant effect on his real income. In contrast, a fall or rise in the price of houses, for instance, may very well be expected to make a consumer significantly better or worse off by changing the effective purchasing power of a fixed money income.

A relevant matter to the relationship between price and quantity demanded is the number of uses to which a good may be put. In general, the greater the number of uses, the larger the change in demand to be expected, for the greater is the scope for extending demand after a price fall (and *vice versa*). Tea, for example, has fewer uses than eggs, so that a fall in the price of tea may be likely to cause a smaller rise in demand than a fall in the price of eggs.

Finally, it should be mentioned that the responsiveness of demand to price changes tends to be larger the longer the time period under consideration. This is true for both rises and falls in price, and reflects the fact that some people often take quite a while even to hear about price changes; and very few people are so flexible that they adjust their habits instantly the price of a good rises or falls.

*Elasticity of demand*

Economists have a special way of measuring the responsiveness of demand to changes in price—they call it **elasticity**. Formally, the elasticity of demand is a fraction (or ratio)—the proportionate change in quantity demanded divided by the proportionate change in price. For a commodity which has many substitutes, and whose demand responds easily to price changes, the fraction is larger than 1, and demand is said to be *elastic*. If a 1 per cent price fall causes a 2 per cent rise in quantity, for example, a good would be in elastic demand.[2]

In contrast, a good which has few substitutes, and for which the demand responds weakly to a price change, would have an elasticity of demand of less than 1, and demand would be said to be *inelastic*. A 5 per cent price fall leading to only a 1 per cent increase in quantity would be an example of this kind of good.

Between the two cases mentioned we may discern a third, bench mark, category, comprising goods for which the demand responds to a given percentage price change by changing in quantity by exactly the same percentage. If demand falls by 1 per cent when the price rises by 1 per cent, the elasticity of demand is said to be equal to *unity*. It is not hard to see that, for such goods, total expenditure on the commodity is identical at all prices. But we may observe that for goods for which the demand is elastic, total expenditure increases as price falls (since demand expands relatively more than price falls). Conversely, for goods for which the demand is inelastic, total expenditure increases as price rises (since demand does not fall off relatively as much as price rises).

## Shifts in demand

We argued earlier that it was often reasonable to make *ceteris paribus* assumptions about factors such as income, tastes, etc., which affect demand. These assumptions were necessary in order that a demand curve might be derived at all. But it does not follow that we must retain the assumptions in our analysis of market behaviour. Suppose in fact, that a change in a *ceteris paribus* assumption occurs. We sometimes refer to such a change as one in the **conditions** of demand. All we need to do is to draw a new demand curve. An example may

2. The most common formula for the calculation of elasticity of demand is:

$$\varepsilon_d = \frac{\text{change in quantity}}{\text{quantity}} \div \frac{\text{change in price}}{\text{price}}$$

So if a fall in price of from £100 to £99 brings about a rise in quantity demanded from 200 to 204:

$$\varepsilon_d = \frac{4}{200} \times \frac{100}{1} = 2$$

help to make the matter clear. Imagine something happening (such as the discovery that ice cream stops baldness) which makes people decide they want to buy more ice cream. We could interpret this change as a shift to the right of the demand curve $DD$ to $D'D'$ in Figure 4.2, implying that *at every price*, the quantity demanded is

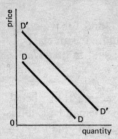

*Figure 4.2* An increase in demand

greater than it was before. A fall in income, on the other hand, might shift the demand curve back again to $DD$, as might an appropriate change in any one of the other determinants of demand.

It must be emphasised that changes in the price of a good itself do *not* shift the demand curve. We read the effects of such price changes by moving *along* the curve. In contrast, changes in the prices of other goods *are* alterations in *ceteris paribus* assumptions. The extent and manner in which they cause the demand curve to shift depends upon the nature of the good in question. A fall in the price of a substitute for a good tends to shift the demand curve downwards —less being bought at every price when there is a cheaper substitute available. But there are also goods which are *complementary* to each other, which tend to be demanded together, and which cause opposite kinds of shifts in demand curves. Tennis racquets and tennis balls are, for example, complements. A fall in the price of racquets tends to shift the demand curve for tennis balls upwards, more balls being demanded as soon as people buy more (cheaper) racquets.

## Supply

Continuing our discussion of the forces acting on market prices, we now shift our attention from demand and look more closely at the determinants of the supply of a commodity. Supply, like demand, depends on many factors. The principal ones are the costs of production, the kind of market in which business operates, and the objectives or goals at which the owners of a business enterprise are aiming.

As we explained in Chapter 2, it is usual in economics to assume, as a first approximation, that firms are in business primarily to maximise profits. Although this is clearly not true in every case, we can safely adopt the assumption here in order to derive certain elementary conclusions about market behaviour. It may need qualification later, when (in more advanced work) alternative goals, such as maximum sales or growth of the business are substituted for it. We assume, too, that the market is a competitive one comprising a large number of small firms. We shall return later in this chapter to consider the implications of this assumption.

Our main concern at the moment, however, is to relate quantities supplied to price. We therefore derive a **market supply schedule,** and corresponding supply curve, for a commodity in which the amounts offered for sale are related to a range of prices. Such a total market schedule for ice cream, for example, would have to be made up of the supply schedules of all the existing and potential ice cream manufacturers. If there were only two firms, their supply schedules might be as shown in Table 4.2. (The numbers are kept deliberately,

Table 4.2   **Supply schedules for ice cream (hypothetical)**
*Quantities supplied per week*

| Price, pence | Firm A | Firm B | Firm A plus Firm B |
|---|---|---|---|
| 1 | 1 | 0 | 1 |
| 2 | 3 | 2 | 5 |
| 3 | 5 | 3 | 8 |
| 4 | 7 | 4 | 11 |
| 5 | 9 | 5 | 14 |
| 6 | 11 | 6 | 17 |
| 7 | 13 | 7 | 20 |
| 8 | 15 | 8 | 23 |

if unrealistically, small.) As in the case of demand we can plot the **supply curves** of each firm on graph paper, adding, once again, the quantities supplied by the two firms together to obtain the market supply curve—Figure 4.3 (i), (ii) and (iii).

In contrast to the demand curves of Figure 4.1, all three of our supply curves slope upwards. This feature of the supply curve is clearly related to the cost structure of firms. If a firm is to be induced to offer additional units of a commodity for sale, it is obvious that the price at which it is able to sell them must cover their costs of production.[3] An upward sloping supply curve implies that the higher the price the larger the quantities that would be offered for sale. The justification for such an upward slope, then, may be that costs rise, at the margin, as output increases. For this reason a rise in price

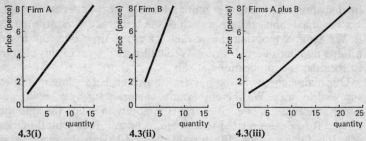

*Figure 4.3* Supply curves for individual firms and the market supply of ice cream per week

may be seen as necessary in order to cover the addition to total costs occasioned by the higher output.

The changes in total costs attributable to changed output are known as extra, or **marginal costs**. We shall assume here that marginal costs in fact rise as output increases, so that we may examine the determination of market price in such a situation. We must realise, however, that if costs do not increase, then the supply curve need not be upward sloping. Some of the implications of dropping this assumption may be quite readily appreciated, but the reader is warned that certain others must await more advanced work in economics.[4]

## Elasticity of supply

Economists are, of course, interested in the extent to which supply reacts to changes in price. The measure of responsiveness adopted is known as the **elasticity of supply**. Similarly defined to the elasticity

3. Costs here are defined to include an element of profit, which economists call 'normal profit', defined as the minimum necessary to persuade a firm to produce in its existing market. Normal profits are related to the opportunity cost of capital —the amount that could be earned by switching resources to an alternative industry.

4. There are even difficulties in drawing a supply curve at all.

of demand, the elasticity of supply is a ratio or fraction—that of the proportionate change in quantity supplied relative to an associated proportionate change in price. For goods where supply responds easily, the fraction has a value in excess of 1, implying that a price fall (or rise) induces a more than proportionate rise (or fall) in the quantity offered for sale, and the good is termed one in *elastic supply*. On the other hand, for goods where supply responds only weakly to changes in price, the fraction has a value of less than 1, and the good is termed one in *inelastic supply*.

When we come to identify the factors responsible for deciding whether elasticity of supply is likely to be great or small for a particular good, the question of the availability of substitutes is of great importance, as it was in the case of demand. Substitutes in supply, however, have a rather different significance. In order for supply to be readily responsive to changes in price there must be ready alternative occupations for factors of production. In other words, there must be goods to or from which production can readily be switched.

Compare, for instance, the supply of plastic toy cars with that of potatoes. In the former case, one might reasonably expect that it was relatively easy for a firm to switch labour and other resources from producing plastic cars to any of an obviously wide range of other plastic toys. The responsiveness of supply to changes in the price of toy cars would, then, tend to be greater than that to a change in the price of potatoes. Once potatoes are planted, there is no scope at all in the short run for a farmer to switch to another crop This example also brings out the point that elasticity of supply, similarly again to that of demand, tends to be greater the longer the time allowed for adjustments to take place.

## Shifts in supply

Supply curves are drawn up on *ceteris paribus* assumptions, to allow the relationship between price and quantity supplied to be isolated. Foremost among those factors which are assumed to remain unchanged over a period are costs of production, behind which lie such matters as the state of technology and the prices of the factors of production used by firms. This assumption does not mean that costs do not vary with output, but that the relationship between costs and output does not change over time. If any change of this kind occurs, we refer to it as a change in the **conditions** of supply. We can deal with it in a similar way to that in which we dealt with shifts in demand. We can move the entire supply curve.

Suppose, for example, a new invention makes possible a lowering of costs of ice creams. We can interpret this as a downward movement of the entire supply curve, as from *SS* to *S'S'* in Figure 4.4, implying that a larger quantity would now be supplied at *every price*.

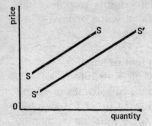

Figure 4.4 An increase in supply

## Market price formation

We have now derived independent relationships between demand and price, and between supply and price. Let us put together the market demand and supply schedules and curves which we invented for ice cream in Tables 4.3 and Figure 4.5. Remember that *DD*

Table 4.3  **Quantities of ice cream demanded and supplied per week**

| Price, pence | Market demand | Market supply |
|---|---|---|
| 8 | 1 | 23 |
| 7 | 2 | 20 |
| 6 | 5 | 17 |
| 5 | 8 | 14 |
| 4 | 11 | 11 |
| 3 | 14 | 8 |
| 2 | 17 | 5 |
| 1 | 20 | 1 |

portrays the quantities that consumers wish to buy at various prices, while *SS* shows the quantities that suppliers wish to offer for sale at the same set of prices.

It can be seen that only when the market price is 4 pence are supply and demand the same—or, to put it another way, that there are no disappointed consumers or suppliers. In such a situation, market price is said to be at an **equilibrium** level.

The meaning and nature of equilibrium can best be understood by examining the likely consequences of any other price obtaining in the market. Suppose, for example, market price were below equilibrium, say at 2 pence, consumers would want to buy 17 ice creams, but only 5 would be offered for sale.

The excess of demand over supply would tend to force the price up towards equilibrium, as consumers competed with each other for the limited supply. Conversely, at a price in the market above the equilibrium, there would be the opposite situation, an excess of

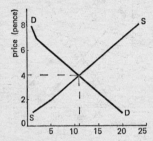

*Figure 4.5* Equilibrium market price, where supply equals demand

supply over demand. At 7 pence for an ice cream for instance, market demand is only 2, whereas 20 would be offered for sale. Market forces on the supply side would now tend to push price downwards, as sellers competed with each other to dispose of their stocks. The market is in equilibrium only where the supply and demand curves intersect, at a price of 4 pence, and with 11 ice creams being bought and sold. Only then is there neither excess demand nor excess supply, with no market forces acting on the price to change it.

## Changes in demand and supply

The framework for the analysis of market price just described has an almost unlimited number of uses in economics. A few illustrations may be given.

Suppose that a market is in equilibrium and there is a change of tastes. Say, for instance, that people start to like ice cream less than they did before.

Readers should be on their guard here against one of the most common mistakes made by beginning students of economics, when they confuse *movements along* with *shifts* of a supply or demand curve. Remember always that a demand curve, or a supply curve, is drawn on *ceteris paribus* assumptions to show the relationship between price and quantity demanded or supplied. If there is a change in one of these assumptions, this means that there is a change in the *conditions* of demand or supply, and the entire curve shifts as the relationship between price and quantity alters at every price. In our example here, the change in tastes is such a change in the conditions of demand, and its effect is to shift the whole demand curve downwards to the left. Since there is, however, no change in

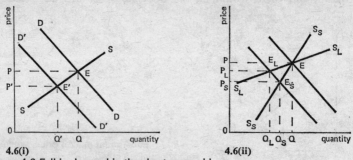

4.6(i)                          4.6(ii)

*Figure* 4.6 Fall in demand in the short run and long run

the conditions of supply, the lower quantity supplied in the new equilibrium situation results only from the fall in price. The supply curve itself does *not* shift.

We can represent the change in the conditions of demand, as in Figure 4.6 (i), as a downward shift of the demand curve for ice cream from $DD$ to $D'D'$. The effect is that the market tends towards a new equilibrium level ($E'$) at the intersection of $SS$ and $D'D'$, where both price and quantity have been reduced, from $OP$ to $OP'$ and from $OQ$ to $OQ'$ respectively.

## Short- and long-run

We can take the analysis one stage further if we remember that supply tends to be more responsive to changes in price the longer the period of time we allow for adjustment. In Figure 4.6 (ii) there are two supply curves going through the original equilibrium point ($E$). $S_SS_S$ is the short period supply curve. $S_LS_L$ is the curve for the longer period. The difference between them is simply that the long run supply curve shows a higher degree of responsiveness of quantity to price—i.e. it is more elastic—than the short run curve. It may be seen too that in the long run a fall in demand tends to have a less depressive effect on price, but a larger effect on sales, than in the short run. Initially, the quantity supplied falls only from $OQ$ to $OQ_S$, causing price to fall from $OP$ to $OP_S$. But as supply falls further in the long run to $OQ_L$, market price partly recovers to $OP_L$.

The influence of time on the demand side can be similarly illustrated. The reader might try to draw for himself a pair of diagrams showing how a decrease in supply, following a rise in costs, can raise price more in the short run than in the long run.

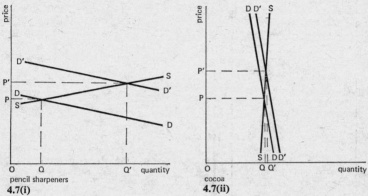

*Figure 4.7* Rise in demand. Elastic and inelastic supply and demand

From the analysis in this section, moreover, we can derive a general conclusion. The more elastic supply and/or demand, the more a change in either of them is likely to lead to changes in quantities bought and sold, and the less to changes in market price. Consider, for example, the two goods in Figure 4.7. In part (i) of the diagram, both the demand for and the supply of pencil sharpeners are assumed to be very responsive to price changes. The rise in demand depicted has a relatively smaller effect on market price than on the equilibrium market quantity demanded and supplied.

In Figure 4.7 (ii), in contrast, the supply of and demand for cocoa are both assumed to be relatively unresponsive to price changes. In this case, the rise in demand is seen to be reflected in a larger change in market price, and a smaller change in market quantity.

## Agricultural markets

We must mention here one important feature of the last diagram, which is in some ways typical of the nature of supply and demand conditions in the market for a number of agricultural products. Supply tends to be inelastic with respect to price changes, at any rate in the short run, because factors such as the weather and the prevalence of disease may be the chief determinants of crop size. Demand, too, tends to be inelastic with respect to price, but tends to rise and fall whenever there are changes in consumers' incomes.

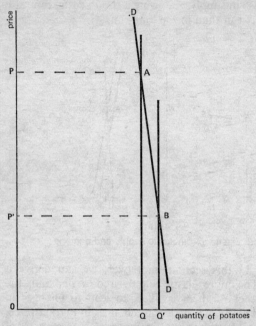

*Figure 4.8* A change in supply, under conditions of inelastic demand, changes total revenue

The implications of inelastic supply and demand in a market are illustrated in Figure 4.8 for an agricultural product, such as potatoes. We assume that good harvest-time weather increases the quantity available for sale from $OQ$ to $OQ'$. The consequences of the larger crop can be seen from the diagram to be serious for potato farmers. Not only is there a substantial fall in price from $OP$ to $OP'$, but total revenue of the farmers falls with the larger crop. Price multiplied by quantity, $OP'$ times $OQ'$, is less than $OP$ times $OQ$. (Or the rectangle $OP'BQ'$ is smaller than $OPAQ$.) This happens *because* demand is inelastic, so that the proportionate rise in quantity sold is less than the proportionate fall in price.

This kind of situation tends to typify the market behaviour for many agricultural products. It is not surprising that, in addition to agriculture being subject to relatively large price fluctuations as crop size varies, farmers' incomes tend also to rise and fall from year to year. Farmers are inclined to be relatively well off when harvests are small, and badly off when they are large. For this reason it is common to find that governments in most countries tend to intervene in agricultural markets with various kinds of schemes to lessen the impact on farmers of short-run market forces, and to stabilise to some extent farm incomes and prices.

## A specific tax

A final example of the use to which supply and demand analysis may be put is to examine the effect of taxation. Suppose the govern-

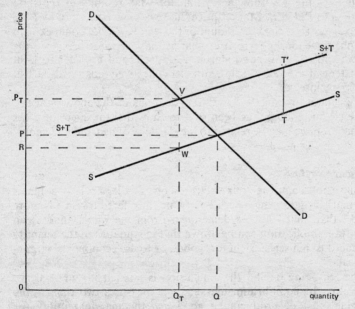

*Figure 4.9* A specific tax; effects on price, quantity, and government revenue

ment decides to impose a tax on matches. What will be the consequences for (a) market price, and (b) sales? And (c) how much revenue will the government obtain?

The answers to these questions are suggested by looking at Figure 4.9. $SS$ and $DD$ are the original supply and demand curves. Market equilibrium is $OQ$ sales at price $OP$. A tax equal to $TT'$ is now imposed. Assume that sellers are given the responsibility of paying this tax to the government. They will no longer be willing to supply the same quantities at the same range of prices as they did before. We can imagine them adding the tax to each price at which they would be willing to supply a given quantity. We can depict this by drawing a new supply curve $(S + T)$ parallel to $SS$, such that the vertical distance between them is equal to the tax itself $(TT')$.

Note that we *cannot* assume that market price also rises by the full amount of the tax. In our diagram it certainly does not do so. When the new equilibrium is reached, market price will be $OP_T$ and sales $OQ_T$. Consumers' total expenditure is $OP_T V Q_T$, which is what suppliers receive. Out of this total, sellers must pay $VW$ $(= TT')$ per unit to the government, so that total tax revenue to the state amounts to $P_T VWR$. Market price, however, has risen only by $PP_T$, which is less than the full amount of the tax $(P_T R)$. We could explain this phenomenon by suggesting that as market price rose when the tax was imposed, demand started to fall off, and in order to limit the extent of the fall in sales, suppliers effectively absorbed part of the tax themselves.

We cannot investigate the full implications of the analysis in this volume,[5] but enough has been said to show that the effect of a tax on market price may be related to the elasticity of demand and supply of a particular good.

### Economic welfare

We have now completed our discussion on the role of prices as signals in a market, indicating whether the amount offered for sale is more or less than that which is demanded. From the whole analysis an important implication can be drawn that in equilibrium the quantity produced is in a sense 'right' or 'good', or to use economists' jargon, **optimal.**

The reasoning behind the conclusion is implicit in our analysis. It is this. In equilibrium, market price measures two things—the marginal cost of producing a good *and* the marginal utility (or satisfaction) obtained by consuming it. Price measures marginal cost because sellers offer an extra good for sale only if it yields a revenue which covers the cost of producing it. Price measures marginal

5. See, however, G. H. Peters, *Private & Public Finance*, Chapter 10, in this series.

utility because (if we assume that consumers try to maximise their satisfaction in disposing of their incomes) buyers purchase an extra good only if it yields enough utility to make the expenditure on it worthwhile. Producers go on offering more of a good for sale if price is greater than marginal cost; consumers continue buying more of a good if price is less than marginal utility. Hence, when price is at an equilibrium level, and is the same for all producers and consumers, we can draw the inference that marginal utility is equal to marginal cost.

We may usefully recall, now, our discussion of the true nature of costs in economics. The opportunity cost of producing a good is the sacrifice made in not producing another good. So the equality of marginal cost and marginal utility at equilibrium means that the benefit derived by consumers from purchasing an extra unit of a good is equal to its cost as measured by the opportunity foregone of having more of another good in its place.

If marginal cost is not equal to marginal utility, satisfaction can clearly be increased by switching resources between products. If marginal utility is greater than marginal cost, it is worth producing more of a commodity because the sacrifice of other goods given up is less than the marginal increase in satisfaction from having more of it. The opposite is true if marginal utility is less than marginal cost. Hence, if marginal cost is brought into equality with marginal utility through the operation of market price, satisfaction of the community cannot be increased by producing more or less of the good. Moreover, if marginal cost is equal to marginal utility in the market for every single good and service, it follows that the distribution of resources is, in a sense, optimal.

## Social institutions

Care must, however, be exercised in interpreting the meaning of the statement that the price mechanism leads to an ideal or optimum distribution of resources. This conclusion follows only if we ignore some of the questions about what underlies the supply and demand schedules which operate as market forces. As was briefly mentioned at the end of the last chapter, such factors as the social and institutional framework within which an economy operates influence supply and demand. We shall consider these influences in greater detail later, but their importance can be grasped by taking one such factor, the distribution of income, as an example.

Suppose we accept a given distribution of income as existing in a country, and allow market price to allocate resources so that marginal utility is equal to marginal cost throughout the economy. Let us further assume that the initial distribution of income was very unequal. We might fairly conclude that the market will succeed in securing the production of a fair amount of champagne, yachts, Rolls-Royce cars, and luxury hotels.

But if we now imagine that it is considered socially desirable to redistribute income more equally by taking from the rich and giving to the poor, it is clear that there will be a shift in demand away from goods of the kinds mentioned above bought by high income groups. Market forces of supply and demand will still operate to shift resources until marginal cost is equal everywhere to marginal utility. But the collection of goods and services now produced is likely to be quite different.

How can we choose between the two distributions of resources brought about by the price mechanism, each of which reflects a different distribution of income in the economy? The answer is that we cannot do so unless we are prepared to choose first which of the two income distributions we consider more desirable. This is a social question, not an economic one. Therefore, we can conclude that the allocation of resources in an economy will be optimal in a full sense, only if we accept that the underlying distribution of income is also optimal.

In the light of this reasoning, we must reinterpret the notion of equilibrium price and output in a more restricted sense. In particular, we must remember that the distribution of resources achieved by market forces assumes a host of underlying social and institutional matters like the distribution of income. If we are prepared to accept all these matters as in a sense desirable, then indeed we can more safely regard the system as securing a 'good' allocation of scarce resources. But if, as economists, we are careful to avoid making value judgments about the desirability of the social and institutional framework within which the economy operates, we must make a much more limited conclusion about the nature of equilibrium— namely, that it is the state of affairs towards which economic forces of supply and demand will tend in the market place. The equilibrium quantity of ice cream, or of anything else, is that quantity which, if produced, leaves no unsatisfied buyers or sellers. But we must remember that supply and demand are really no more than 'catch-alls', behind which lie all the social forces which may influence them. We shall return to discuss these and other matters, which must be considered before passing judgment on the efficiency of the pricing system, in Chapter 8.

## Competition

We must make one final observation about the implications of market analysis for economic welfare, one which is related to a different aspect of economic behaviour.

Most of the present chapter has been based on the assumption that the market we are concerned with is a **competitive** one. However, in the real world there are a variety of market situations in which a firm may find itself. At one extreme there is a highly competitive state of affairs, wherein a large number of small producers each sell a commodity which is no different from that of any other producer and there is complete freedom of entry for firms into the industry. In such circumstances no single seller can *by himself* influence price in the market by withholding supplies; he is too small. Such a market is dubbed **perfectly competitive** in economics. And although it may be rare enough in the real world, it provides a useful reference base against which other market situations may be compared.

In many cases, moreover, a single seller *can* significantly affect market price by altering the quantity which he puts on the market. He may be the only producer, a **monopolist**, or there may be only a small number of oligopolists (from the Greek words meaning 'few sellers'), or the public may feel some brand loyalty to his product, perhaps because of advertising, which enables him to charge a higher price for it than that which other producers are able to charge for goods of that kind.

The analysis of a firm's behaviour under conditions of **imperfect competition** are complex, and cannot be considered closely here.[6] We may, however, note one vitally important difference between the position of a profit-maximising monopolist and that of a firm in perfect competition. While the latter can sell as much of his product as he likes at the ruling market price, the monopolist is, by definition, so large that he can only succeed in selling additional quantities by lowering price. Moreover, since only one price can normally exist in a market for the same commodity, when the monopolist lowers price to sell another unit, he must lower it on *all* the units that he sells.

The implications of this feature on the output policy of a firm can be understood by reconsidering what is meant by our earlier statement that a seller offers goods for sale up to the point where the price he gets for them covers his marginal costs. This is true for the firm under perfect competition, because the price he receives is only another way of saying the increase in revenue he obtains from selling an additional unit. Economists call the change in receipts following

6. See Gordon Hewitt, *Economics of the Market*.

an increase in the quantity sold **marginal revenue**. It is defined as the total revenue from the sale of $n$ units, minus the total revenue from the sale of $(n - 1)$ units.

For a small firm in perfect competition, marginal revenue is equal to price. But for a monopolist, the sale of an extra unit of a good is only attainable by reducing price, not only for the additional unit, but for all the goods sold. In other words, marginal revenue is always

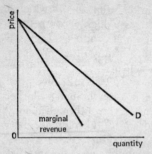

Figure 4.10 Marginal revenue under imperfect competition

less than price, and we can draw a marginal revenue curve which lies below the demand curve, as in Figure 4.10.

An example may help to make the matter clear. Suppose a large firm can sell 60 units at a price of £1·00 each, but in order to sell 61 units the price must be lowered to 99 pence. The increase in total revenue which the monopolist receives from the 101st sale is not 99 pence but 39 pence. He adds 99 pence by selling one more unit at 99 pence but loses 1 pence on each of the 60 previous sales. In other words, his marginal revenue of 39 pence is the total revenue from 101 units (61 × 99 pence) *minus* the total revenue from 100 units (60 × 100 pence).

Whereas we said earlier that a firm produces up to the point where marginal cost is equal to price, we now know this really meant: up to the point where the extra cost was just covered by the extra receipts—i.e. where marginal cost equals marginal revenue. Although price and marginal revenue are the same for a firm in perfect competition, the monopolist, as we have seen, finds that marginal revenue is less than price. Hence, he maximises profits by producing *less* than the competitive output. In Figure 4.11 the equilibrium position is where the monopolist produces an output of $OA$, i.e. where the marginal cost curve cuts the marginal revenue curve. Competitive output, where marginal cost equals marginal utility, would be $OB$.

Note, however, that the monopolist is able to sell $OA$ in the market at a price $OP$, which is in excess of marginal revenue. If we retain the assumption that price measures marginal utility to the consumer of a good, we must draw the implication that monopoly equilibrium tends to result in marginal utility being greater than marginal cost, and that an increase in output would add more to consumer satisfaction than to costs. And since costs in economics are opportunity

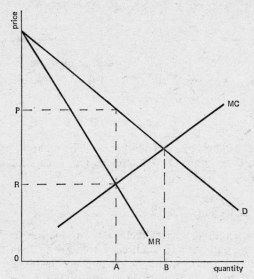

*Figure 4.11* Monopoly equilibrium

costs, *prima facie*, resources used in the output of a good produced in such circumstances involve, at the margin, a sacrifice of other goods of less value than the satisfaction that they provide to consumers.

We may conclude that the presence of monopolistic elements in a market tends to lead to less production than would occur under competition; and that (by the standards which we applied for judging the efficiency of the price mechanism for allocating resources) output is, *ceteris paribus*, less than optimal. However, we must not jump to the conclusion that such a state of affairs is necessarily undesirable, for reasons which are discussed in Chapter 7, when we consider economic policy in general.

We have now completed our discussion of the way in which supply and demand operate in the market for goods. The methods of analysis used are, however, generally applicable to many kinds of situation. In the following chapter we shall extend them by considering the way in which they operate in other kinds of market.

# Chapter 5

# Supply and Demand in other Markets

The purpose of this chapter is to analyse the working of the price mechanism in three types of market situation, namely:

i. Markets for factors of production.
ii. Financial markets.
iii. International markets.

In all three types, the general principles of supply and demand apply, but each possesses sufficient individual characteristics to call for brief separate treatment.

### Markets for factors of production

As we know from Chapter 2, the term 'factors of production' is given to all resources—labour, capital, land, etc.—that are used in the production of goods and services. Here we shall concentrate on one—labour—and use it to illustrate our discussion of the determination of the prices of factors of production.

The labour market is where the *price of labour*, commonly called its wage, is determined. We must look here if we want an explanation of why men are paid more, on average, in the car industry than in the building trade; why wages are higher in London than in Belfast; why women earn less than men; why doctors are paid more than clerks; and so on.

The wage rate for any occupation is, in essence, no different from any other price. We should, therefore, be correct in thinking that it is determined by the forces of supply and demand for labour. Our task now is merely to identify distinguishing features of the labour market which express themselves either on the demand side or on the supply side.

### The demand for labour

The nature of demand in the market for labour differs in one important respect from that for a commodity. Labour is not wanted directly for itself, but for what it is capable of producing. For this reason, we usually speak of the demand for labour's services as being **derived** from the demand for the good or service which it helps to produce. Labour, of course, is generally combined with other factors of production—capital, land, and raw materials.

The way in which economists normally approach the demand for labour by a business is by focusing attention on the **productivity** of the labour employed. In the *short run*, a firm may have a fixed amount of capital equipment which may be used together with a variable number of workers. If men are added one at a time to its labour force, the firm can observe the effect on total output. The difference in total production which results from employing an additional man is known as the **marginal product of labour**. When the marginal product is valued at the price at which it sells in the goods market, we obtain a measure of the marginal product in terms of money. It is this marginal product which is regarded as the demand for labour.

Consider the following example. Imagine that a firm, working with its fixed land and capital, obtains total outputs of turnips from men as shown in Table 5.1. The figures are, as usual, hypothetical.

Table 5.1 shows that one man working on an acre of land produces

Table 5.1 **Turnip output per week on 1 acre of land**

| Men employed | Total production (Tons) | Marginal product (Tons) |
| --- | --- | --- |
| 1 | 2 | 2 |
| 2 | 5 | 3 |
| 3 | 9 | 4 |
| 4 | 12 | 3 |
| 5 | 14 | 2 |
| 6 | 15 | 1 |
| 7 | 15½ | ½ |

2 tons of turnips. When a second man is added, total output rises by 3 tons to 5. Marginal product is, therefore, 2 tons in physical terms. To find the marginal product in money terms, we need to know its market value. If we assume that turnips sell for, say, £10 per ton, the last column in the table can be interpreted as £20, £30, £40, £30, £20, £10, and £5 worth of output.

Let us plot the curve of marginal product on a graph as in

Figure 5.1. It can be seen to rise at first and then to fall. The tendency for marginal product to fall when units of a **variable factor** are added to a **fixed factor** is known as **the law of diminishing returns**. It is thought to be of widespread application, and lies behind much of the argument that costs of production often tend to rise after a certain amount of output is reached. This tendency is, however, of limited importance in the present context. Our immediate task is rather to explain why the curve of marginal product is said to *be* the demand curve of the firm for labour in the short run.

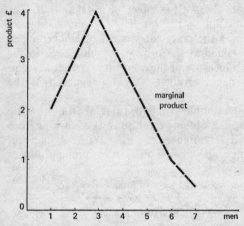

*Figure 5.1* Diminishing returns to a variable factor of production

The reason is simple enough. Firms are assumed to be in business to make a profit. Provided the employment of an extra man adds more to revenue than to costs, it pays to employ him. Suppose the wage rate is £10 per week. It is obviously profitable to employ one man, since he adds £20 to total revenue of the firm. A second man adds £30, a third £40, and so on. It is worth engaging six men in fact, but a seventh man costs the firm £10, but only adds £5 worth of turnips to total revenue. So we can read the curve of marginal product in Figure 5.1 as being, in effect, the demand curve for labour of the firm.

The *total* market demand curve for labour is obtained by adding together the demand curves of individual firms in a similar way to that used in the goods market to derive the total demand curve for a commodity. (See Figure 4.1, page 56.) The resulting curve may be drawn in this manner for either the short run or the long run. The only difference is that in the long period a firm is able to vary the employment of other factors of production so that it may not alter the proportions in which factors are employed. While this means that the law of diminishing returns need not apply,[1] it does not significantly affect the interpretation of the marginal product curve as the (derived) demand for labour.

A final point to be made about the nature of the demand curve for a factor of production, is that it is important to specify the degree of competition obtaining in the market. In fact, we have really assumed so far that firms are in competition for labour, and that no one of them is large enough to influence the wage rate by restricting the number of men it employs. This is the same kind of assumption that we made initially when dealing with supply and demand in goods markets. If the labour market operates under conditions of imperfect competition, we must modify the analysis in the manner described at the end of the last chapter. This may modify also some of the conclusions reached, but we must refer the reader to a later volume in this series for a full treatment of this subject.[2]

## The supply of labour

Let us now consider the supply side of the labour market. We must first distinguish between the amount of work offered by an individual, and the total labour market supply of all workers. As far as an individual person is concerned, the amount of work he is prepared to do is likely to be related to the wage rate that he can command. He may be prepared to give up more hours of leisure as the rate rises, and in doing so he is really substituting work for time off. In other words, we are witnessing the operation of the substitution effect of a rise in price, which we observed earlier (see pages 57–58) in connection with the demand for a commodity by a consumer.

A price change, it will be remembered, has an income effect as well as a substitution effect. From the viewpoint of the supply of labour, a rise in the wage rate, while the prices of goods and services are held constant, can be said to signify an increase in real income. Now, the effect of a rise in real income on the supply of effort is, on the whole, likely to operate in the direction of a reduction in supply. This is because a rise in income tends to be associated with an increased capacity to enjoy leisure.

1. Varying the quantity of inputs while keeping the proportions between them fixed, is known as changing the *scale* of production.
2. Gordon Hewitt, *Economics of the Market*.

So we are faced with very uncertain consequences of a change in wage rates, and no general rules are applicable. A rise in the wage rate may lead either to an increase or to a reduction in the supply of effort. The tendency to *substitute* work for leisure is countered by an increased demand for leisure associated with rising real income. We know only that if the net effect of a rise in the wage rate is an increase in supply, then the substitution effect must be greater than the income effect. The supply curve would slope upwards, as usual, and

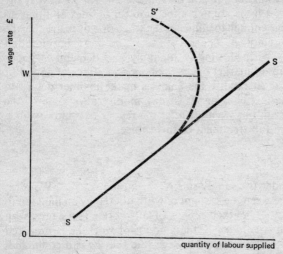

*Figure 5.2* Supply curve of labour

have an appearance like that of *SS* in Figure 5.2. If, on the other hand, the income effect predominates, a rise in wage rates will lead to a reduction in work effort. The supply curve would then 'bend backwards', as does the broken curve *SS'* in Figure 5.2, indicating that as wage rates rise beyond *OW*, the supply of work effort falls off.

We may well ask, now, one question. Which is the 'true' supply curve, *SS* or *SS'*? In order to provide an answer, we need to observe whether men work more or less when their wage rate rises. In the real world, unfortunately, the evidence pertaining to actual behaviour in response to wage rate variations is not easy to interpret. It seems clear that some supply curves of labour do slope normally upwards while others may bend back, at least over a certain range of wage rates. In considering the response of labour to a change of wage rates, however, it should not be forgotten that the extent to which *individuals* are free to vary their working hours is quite restricted in normal situations.

As mentioned earlier, we must be careful to distinguish between the reactions of an individual to a change in the wage rate and reactions of a number of workers as implied in the market supply curve. The latter is a good deal more likely to have a normal upward slope. For any occupation, an increase in wage rates tends to attract workers from other occupations, and this effect may swamp any inclination on the part of existing workers to work fewer hours. Indeed, if one ignores differences in individual skill and ability, so regarding labour as a **homogeneous** factor of production, one might even expect that market forces would tend towards equality of wage rates in all occupations. If wage rates differed and workers were free to move, there would be a natural inclination to switch from low paid to high paid jobs. Such shifts in the labour supply to different occupations would act as equilibrating forces. They would clearly be greater in the long run than in the short.

## *Wage differentials*

Of course, the world is not like this. Wage rates vary considerably between different occupations, a fact for which there are several possible explanations. First, labour is not homogeneous. Skill and ability differentials are reflected in different marginal productivities. Moreover, some people prefer hard work (not to mention risk) to an easy life, and the market may reward them accordingly. Second, labour is not free to move from job to job. Mobility is costly and many people prefer to stay in their own locality or with their old workmates in low paid jobs than to move around looking for the best paid occupations. It is true that an excess demand for a certain kind of skill tends to work, through a high wage, to encourage people to train to acquire an appropriate qualification. But an increase in supply may not be forthcoming for years. Third, there are said to be what are called **non-pecuniary advantages and disadvantages** of particular occupations, and they should be notionally added to the wage rate to obtain a realistic picture of the full reward for each job. Assembly line workers in a noisy factory have a relatively unpleasant job, and must therefore be paid enough to ensure a sufficient supply. Farm workers, on the other hand, often seem actually to enjoy their work in the open air. This is probably part of the reason why their wages tend to be well below the average of other industries.

The fourth and final reason why wage rates do not tend everywhere to equality is to be found in the existence of **trade unions**. These associations of workers in an industry or occupation have, as one of their prime purposes, the task of trying to secure high wages for their members. In so far as a trade union can regulate the labour supply by restricting entry into the occupation it controls, it can achieve this quite effectively. In Figure 5.3, for instance, the free

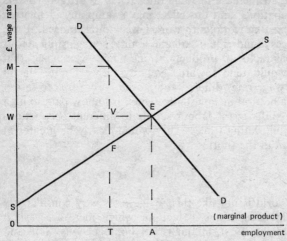

*Figure 5.3* The effect of trade union activity on wage rates and employment

market price of labour would be $OW$, with $OA$ men employed. But a trade union might be able, by acting as a monopolist, to restrict the supply of labour to $OT$, and so secure a wage rate of $OM$. Note that if the union could not control entry into the industry, it could still bargain with employers for a wage of $OM$. The disadvantage of a high wage rate would then be the existence of unemployment, to the extent $AT$. Such a fall in the level of employment in the industry could perhaps be prevented if it were also possible to increase productivity and so effectively shift the demand (marginal productivity) curve upwards.[3]

*Transfer earnings and economic rent*

The wage that must be paid in order to attract a worker to a job must be at least as high as that which he could get in his next most

3. There may be considerable uncertainty, in practice, about the precise value of the marginal product of labour, and this may itself prevent unemployment.

remunerative occupation, which is called his **transfer earnings**—another term for what is effectively the opportunity cost to him of working in a given job. An upward sloping supply curve of labour implies that transfer earnings vary between individuals. Look, for example, at Figure 5.4. The supply curve, *SS*, implies that one man would work at a wage of *OT*, another at a wage of *OV*, another at a wage of *OW*, and so forth. In other words, one man has transfer earnings of *OT*, another of *OV*, and another of *OW*, etc.

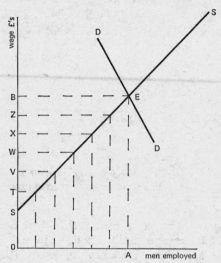

*Figure 5.4* Economic rent (*BES*). The difference between the wage bill (*OBEA*) and total transfer earnings (*OSEA*)

Let us suppose that the demand curve for labour cuts the supply curve at point *E*, and that the equilibrium wage *OB* is paid to all, *OA*, workers. The (*OA*th) man who finds it marginally attractive to work in this occupation has zero transfer earnings. But all other workers receive a wage in excess of their transfer earnings—the man who would offer his services at a wage of *OT* receives an excess of *TB* over his transfer earnings; the man with transfer earnings of *OV* receives an excess of *VB*, etc. The difference between the wage received and the transfer earnings of an individual is a kind of economic surplus, and is sometimes known by the special name of **economic rent**. In the diagram, the economic rent earned by all workers in the industry is *BES* (i.e. the wage bill—*OBEA*, minus total transfer earnings—*OSEA*).

The concept of economic rent relates not only to labour but to any factor of production which has an upward sloping supply curve. If a factor is in fixed (i.e. perfectly inelastic) supply, the supply curve is a vertical straight line, implying that the same amount would be offered for sale at any price. This means that a price of even zero would not reduce the quantity supplied. Hence, the whole payment to the factor would consist of economic rent, which does not need to be paid, on economic grounds, in order to secure its being offered

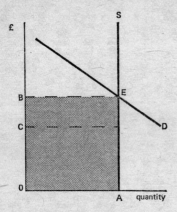

*Figure* 5.5 Economic rent, as the total return to a factor of production in fixed supply

for sale. In Figure 5.5, the equilibrium market price is *OB*, where the quantity demanded, *OA*, is equal to the quantity supplied. However, *OA* would also be supplied at any other price, e.g. at a price of *OC*, or even of zero. The total return to the factor, *OBEA*, thus consists of economic rent.

The factor land is, to all intents and purposes, fixed in supply. This fact gave the American economist, Henry George, in the last century, the idea that the government could impose a tax on land without causing any reduction in the quantity in use.[4] The fairness of taxing land owners in this manner is, of course, quite a separate issue, but it is important to understand this case for imposing a tax on a factor in fixed supply on purely economic grounds.

Note, however, that the argument holds only in the case of land if the tax is universally imposed on this factor. If only farm land, for

4. It is important to note that the economic argument for a tax on land does not involve taxing *improvements*, such as buildings. This might affect the supply of factors of production which are used to make the improvements, and tend to cause such factors to shift into other industries or occupations which were not subject to the tax.

example, were taxed, there would tend to be a reduction in supply, because land would be shifted to other uses, e.g. for building purposes. In other words, there is a real opportunity cost of employing land in one use rather than another, which consists of its transfer earnings in the alternative use.

## Financial markets

The second kind of market to be considered is that where the prices of **financial assets** are determined.

### The nature of financial assets

When we think of the output of an economy, we may be conscious, in the first place, of quantities of goods and services produced by businesses and bought by consumers. But on further reflection, these flows may be regarded not only as physical goods but as **money** payments that are made for them. In a sense money is simply a shadow or counterpart of the physical outputs—a way of measuring them in value terms.

However, money is wanted by some people for its own sake. If you have money, you can regard it as an asset of a financial kind, even if you do not think of spending it immediately. Money has, as it were, a life of its own. And it may be regarded, therefore, as a financial asset which has a value because it can be exchanged for goods and services at any time.

There are, moreover, several other kinds of financial asset as well as money. They include **claims** to the ownership of real property, which often take the form of a piece of paper, such as the deeds of a house; shares in a public company, which are wanted because they entitle the owner to a portion of the future profits of a business; and I.O.U.'s and promissory notes, which give the holder the right to an eventual monetary reward.

People like to keep a part of their wealth in real assets such as a house and its contents; and part in financial assets by holding money in the bank or in a building society, or buying shares in a public company. As we shall see, a complex economy such as that of Britain cannot function efficiently without some of these financial assets and social institutions, such as banks, which have grown up to deal with them. Before continuing with the analysis of the price mechanism in financial markets, we must pause and look briefly at what the economist means by money.

## Money as a medium of exchange

A money system avoids the need for direct barter of goods against goods. If you have a radio you wish to exchange for a camera, you will find it much easier to make an indirect sale for money, which you then use to buy a camera, than to advertise in the hope that you will find someone with exactly the opposite complementary wants to your own. Money is said, in this case, to act as a **medium of exchange**.

This prime function of money is of outstanding importance in the process of production.[5] It means, too, that a business can pay its workers with money which they can then use to buy the varieties of goods and services that they need, instead of having to pay them with bricks, steel tubes, or whatever the company happens to produce. It is not surprising, therefore, to learn that economists regard money as a vital 'lubricant' in the economic system, allowing specialisation to a high degree by avoiding the need for individual workers (and companies) to be paid in quantities of their own physical outputs.

To the man in the street, money is quite simply notes and coin which he can use to buy whatever he needs. To the economist, money is both these things, but it is something very much wider as well, and consists of anything which acts as a medium of exchange by being immediately *acceptable* in settlement of debt.

In primitive societies, valuable goods like gemstones, and even cattle, performed the functions of money, but these are very inconvenient articles as they tend to be bulky, if not risky, to carry about. Consequently, certain *tokens* were developed to take their place. In modern times, these tokens take the form of notes and coins—which belong to the group of financial assets already mentioned—and they are exchangeable for goods and services at current prices.

All financial assets are, however, not equally acceptable in the settlement of debts. Those which are immediately exchangeable into a form which can be used as a means of payment are said to possess the quality of **liquidity**. And the most perfectly liquid assets *are* what we mean by money. The economist, therefore, tends to count as parts of the money supply not only notes and coin but also deposits held in bank accounts.

As readers of another volume in this series will find out,[6] bank deposits are not fully backed by notes in banks' safes, but are scarcely

5. Money has other functions—to act as a store of value and a unit of account.
6. G. H. Peters, *Private and Public Finance*.

more than book-keeping entries in a ledger. One bank customer with say, £100 standing to his credit may transfer all or part of his holding to someone else simply by drawing a cheque instructing the bank to transfer the sum stated on the cheque to a 'payee' to whom he owes money. If the payee happens to have an account at the same bank, it is obvious that there is no need for anything more than a pair of ledger entries, one debit and one credit. But even if the payee banks elsewhere, it may be readily appreciated that, *for the banking system as a whole*, transfers may cancel out and only book-keeping remains to be done.

We cannot indulge here in an explanation of the working of a modern banking system, but we can appreciate that the use of the cheque system for settling debts means that bank deposits must be counted as very liquid assets, and therefore as part of the money supply.

## *The price of financial assets*

Our preliminary discussion of the nature of financial assets may seem remote from the kind of analysis of price determination that the reader has been led to expect. Yet there is a clear relevance which will shortly become apparent. The key to the understanding of the way in which the prices of financial assets are determined is, as might be supposed, to be found in the nature of the demand for and supply of them.

We may approach the subject of deriving a supply curve by thinking of an individual contemplating making a loan of £100 for a year. The argument is not affected by the person or institution to which he lends his money, but for purposes of illustration we may suppose that he lends to another individual, receiving in return a paper I.O.U., or promise of repayment a year hence.

The question of whether or not our individual will supply a loan of £100 is related fundamentally to the notion of opportunity cost. What, we may ask, would he give up if he made the loan? In other words, what is its opportunity cost?

There are an almost infinite number of answers to this question, reflecting the large number of uses to which £100 might otherwise be put. We may, however, concentrate on two of them. First, the £100 could be kept in the form of money, as a liquid asset. Second, it could be spent on consumer goods and services of one sort or another. Hence, another way of putting the same question is to ask why he should sacrifice consumption goods, or even liquidity, in return for the ownership of a non-liquid financial asset (a post-dated I.O.U.).

The answer to the question put in this manner is almost certainly known to you already. Lending money is made financially attractive by the payment of **interest**, usually described as a rate per cent on the sum borrowed. The rate of interest is the price of lending and borrowing. It is the reward that is received for parting with liquidity and it is therefore, in a sense, the price of holding money. At the same time, it is the compensation that is paid for foregoing present consumption, i.e. for saving. If a holder of an I.O.U., worth £100 a year hence, wishes to obtain cash, he may sell the I.O.U. at a discount. If the market rate of interest happens to be 5 per cent he will get £95 for it. £5 is the cost of having £100 now.

### Supply and demand for 'loanable funds'

Our next task is to examine the nature of the forces which determine the rate of interest in markets where lending and borrowing takes place, and which are sometimes described in economic theory by the composite term—the market for *loanable funds*. As usual, we shall find it helpful to look in turn at the supply and the demand side.

(i) *Supply*. We have already suggested that the supply of funds for lending depends partly on the rate of interest. We implied that the

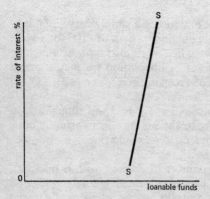

*Figure 5.6* Supply curve of loanable funds

two were positively associated, i.e. that a rise in the rate of interest is accompanied by an increase in the supply of loanable funds, and vice versa. More people tend to enter the market in order to lend money when interest rates rise, for example, and existing lenders are inclined to lend more. In terms of a diagram, this implies an upward sloping curve, such as *SS* in Figure 5.6.

The reader will no doubt have observed that the curve is drawn in such a way as to imply that the responsiveness of supply to changes in the rate of interest is limited. The evidence suggests that this may often be true. The reason can be appreciated if we interpret the supply curve as comprising any sources of funds for lending, whether derived from saving out of current income, accumulated savings from the past held in a liquid form, or simply increases in the quantity of money in the economy. Each of these elements in the supply of loanable funds may react differently to changes in the rate of interest. In so far as the total quantity of money (notes and coin and bank deposits) depends mainly on government policy (see below), and the level of saving depends largely upon income, we may expect the influence of the rate of interest to be small.

(ii) *Demand*. The demand for loanable funds comes from persons and institutions who are short of ready cash for immediate purchases, because, for example, people want to spend more than their income during the current year, to purchase a durable consumer good, like a house, a car, or furniture. There is, however, a second and important element in the demand for loans. This does not come from persons, but from businesses, who need to borrow for the purchase of capital goods, as we have learnt to call them. It is well known that capital intensive techniques of production are more efficient in many lines of output than labour intensive ones. There are literally thousands of examples of this around us. Farming with tractors and combine harvesters raises agricultural output. Machinery of all kinds increases productive potential in the manufacture of cars, washing machines, clocks, pencils—indeed, in virtually every kind of manufacturing activity. Hence, there is a demand for loans from businesses to invest in capital goods to increase production.[7]

Before we can construct a demand curve to go with our supply curve of loanable funds, we must ask the question: How responsive is the demand for loans to changes in the rate of interest? Again we must admit that there are many factors which affect the demand by borrowers for loans, so that the influence of a single one—the rate of interest—may be insignificant. The evidence culled from business behaviour shows that there is, indeed, considerable doubt about the

7. There is also a demand for loans of money for purely speculative purposes about which students of economics must learn later, but which need not worry us at this stage.

extent to which businesses respond to rises in the rate of interest by reducing the amount that they borrow. A tendency for response to be low reflects the fact that the profit to be earned by borrowing in order to build a new factory or to buy a new machine has a distinct air of uncertainty about it. The returns from an investment accrue only in the future, which is unknown and, to a degree, unknowable. Forecasting future profits following the installation of a new machine, for example, depends upon estimating future sales of the goods that can be produced over its entire life, as well as upon trying to guess whether or not the machine will be rendered obsolete quickly by

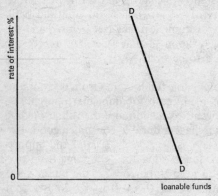

*Figure 5.7* Demand curve for loanable funds

some new invention. In view of uncertainties like these, we may be rather doubtful about the precise relationship between interest rates and the demand for loanable funds. At the same time, it seems reasonable enough to suggest that the lower the rate of interest, the larger the amount of borrowing that persons and businesses may wish to do for all purposes. So we draw a downward sloping demand curve for loanable funds in Figure 5.7.

In the absence of firm evidence to the contrary, we may justify this shape for the curve by the following argument. Imagine that businesses are faced with a schedule of possible investments which they might, in principle, make. These investments may be listed in descending order of (expected) profitability, expressed as a (percentage) rate of return on the cost of the capital good (representing the sum which needs to be borrowed). One investment of £1,000 might be expected to yield a 25 per cent return. Another, slightly less profitable, might yield 22 per cent, a third 20 per cent, and so forth.

It would then appear to be sensible for a business to borrow at a rate of interest of, say, 10 per cent, if it could use the funds to earn anything more than that rate. We can then interpret the demand curve for loanable funds as being derived, on the business side, from a schedule of the rate of return on investments. The parallel with the demand curve for labour as a factor of production is quite close.

### Determination of the rate of interest

Let us now put together in Figure 5.8 the supply and demand curves for loanable funds discussed above. We may observe that the equilibrium rate of interest in the market ($OR$) is that at which the supply

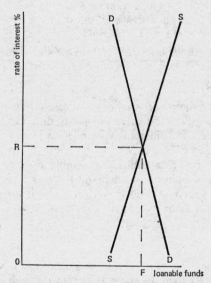

*Figure 5.8* Determination of the rate of interest

and demand for loanable funds, for all purposes, are equal ($OF$). All the general rules about market price are applicable. If the rate of interest is above equilibrium, there will be excess supply, and disappointed lenders may compete to force the rate down. If the rate of interest, on the other hand, is below equilibrium, there will be excess demand, and disappointed borrowers may force the rate up. Moreover, all the range of potential determinants of the supply of and demand for loanable funds, other than the rate of interest, can be brought into the analysis in exactly the same way as that in which we dealt with changes in *ceteris paribus* assumptions in the goods market—by shifting the appropriate supply or demand curve. For example, if there were an increase in the quantity of money, this could be interpreted as a shift of the entire supply curve to the right, because it would imply that the amount of lending on offer at a given rate of interest would be larger than before the change. A rise in income leading to more saving, or a reduction in the public's desire to hold cash as a liquid asset, could be treated in a similar way.

Alternatively, suppose that there were a burst of new inventions making business men anxious to undertake new investments, or merely an improvement in their confidence about the outlook for existing investments, or that the population increased in such a way as to raise the demand for houses for which families wanted loans. Every one of these changes implies an increase in the demand for loanable funds at every rate of interest. Each could therefore be represented by a shift of the entire demand curve to the right.

### The structure of interest rates

We cannot take the analysis of the determination of interest rates further, but the point must be made that there are many different rates of interest ruling in markets for different types of loan in this country. In so far as the duration of a loan, or the risk attached to it varies, we can treat each as being determined in a more or less separate market with a specific supply of and demand for loans of that type. A whole structure of interest rates may then be built up for short, medium, and long term loans with varying degrees of risk.

### Monetary policy

A final word must be said on the topic of interest rates, related to the control that may be exercised over them by the government through what is called **monetary policy**. The full significance of this subject will only be made clear after the next two chapters have been understood, but we may usefully anticipate one major conclusion. The level of total national spending in a country like Britain is liable to fluctuate in the absence of any deliberate policies designed to prevent it.

Fluctuations in aggregate spending involve similar variations in the size of the national income, and it is not difficult to understand that the government may wish to keep these to a minimum. Any instrument which can control components of total expenditure may help. In particular, we may observe that the level of business expenditure on investment may be stimulated or discouraged by movements in interest rates. In so far as investment expenditure is prone to quite erratic changes, therefore, the government may reasonably consider making changes in the quantity of money, in order to influence interest rates and the level of business investment.

The institution which helps in the task of putting monetary policy into effect for the government is the Bank of England. The Bank has several techniques open to it. One is directed towards encouraging or discouraging private commercial banks from making loans to their customers. A bank makes loans by allowing customers, such as businesses, to run up debit overdrafts, which are used to pay creditors. It follows therefore that total bank deposits tend to rise when overdraft lending is increasing (and vice versa). Since we have emphasised earlier that the quantity of money in a country should be taken to include deposits in bank accounts, an increase in their volume is tantamount to an increase in the quantity of money. And we argued above that a change in the money supply would tend to affect the market rate of interest.

A second way of attempting to influence investment expenditure is by directly altering the rate of interest itself. The Bank of England has the power to set certain key rates of interest, which by tradition are linked to other rates in the economy.[8] In the past, the Bank has raised (or lowered) certain notes of interest in order to induce a fall (or rise) in the level of investment; but this kind of policy went out of favour in 1971.

The Bank of England is a nationalised concern, and the important task of trying to influence total investment spending in the economy is therefore under the surveillance of the government. The effectiveness of monetary policy in achieving its goal is, however, subject to controversy. In view of the doubts expressed earlier about the responsiveness of investment decisions by businesses to changes in the rate of interest, this should not be surprising. But when the Bank of England announces a rise in interest rates, the move itself may be taken as a sign by the business community that the government intends to try to reduce investment spending. A reinforcing element may then be introduced, if business confidence about future trade prospects declines. Hence a fall in investment may ensue, even though a change in interest rates alone (i.e. with unchanged confidence) might be ineffective.

8. Reference should be made here to G. H. Peters, *Private and Public Finance*, Chapter 6.

Finally, it is clear that monetary policy is not entirely symmetrical in its effects in raising and lowering investment expenditure. Although a sufficiently restrictive monetary policy, reducing the quantity of money and forcing interest rates up, can eventually always succeed in dampening spending, the reverse is not necessarily true. The rate of interest simply cannot be forced down indefinitely,[9] and it is obvious that no matter how much money is created, people must be induced to spend it before any increase in investment expenditure can take place. If confidence declines in keeping with increases in the quantity of money, all that may happen is that people hoard the extra money rather than spend it. We return to such questions of policy in Chapter 8.

## International markets

Finally we deal, only very briefly, with the third kind of market situation—international markets. This is not because they lack importance. Quite the contrary. Britain derives about a quarter of its entire national income from foreign trade, and the subject is of such importance that a special volume in this series is devoted to international economics.[10]

The brevity of our treatment is, rather, a reflection of the fact that the existence of national political boundaries does not significantly affect the analysis of supply and demand that we have applied to other markets. The two prime economic consequences of the existence of different countries are that factors of production tend to move much less freely across national frontiers than within them; and that every sovereign state usually decides to organise and control a currency of its own, pounds, francs, marks, dollars, etc.

### Comparative cost differences

Consider, first, the implications arising from restricted mobility of factors of production. Our understanding of the way in which factor markets work suggests that factor prices (wages, rents, etc.) might differ significantly between countries because of their differing supplies of factors of production (e.g. of labour and land). Within a country, we might expect factors to move in response to regional price differences; but in so far as mobility is restricted, international

9. A negative real rate of interest would mean that people pay others to allow them to lend them money.

10. H. Katrak, *International Trade and the Balance of Payments*.

trade is something of a substitute for the movement of factors of production. Each country tends to specialise to some extent in goods for whose production its factor endowments make it efficient relative to other goods. Provided that transport costs are not too great, these goods are then exported in exchange for imports of goods in which other countries have a relative advantage.[11] Note, incidentally, the deliberate use of the word *relative* here. If a country can produce both shirts and boots more cheaply than other countries, but its cost advantage is relatively greater in boot production, it can still pay that country to obtain shirts from abroad by exchanging them for boots, which it can make at even lower cost. This is known as the **Principle of Comparative Costs.** In the long run a country must export in order to import. Market forces of supply and demand exert an influence on price levels so that a country finds both exports and imports are profitable, and there is therefore a gain from trading with others.

Let us consider next the significance of the fact that every nation values its output in terms of its own national currency. This poses at once the question of the value of each currency in terms of other currencies—i.e. their prices, or the **rate of exchange** between them. Supply and demand come into play in the determination of exchange rates, and there are no very special differences, in principle, between market forces here and elsewhere. Consider, for example, the rate of exchange between the pound sterling and the dollar.

We can, as usual, construct demand and supply curves. The demand for dollars comes, among other sources, from British importers of U.S. goods, from persons, companies and others who want to invest in the U.S.A., or who wish to buy services provided by Americans, e.g. by travelling in U.S. ships or on U.S. airlines. If the prices of American goods are regarded as fixed in terms of dollars, then the lower the price of dollars in terms of pounds, the more dollars will be demanded. In other words, at an exchange rate of $1 = 40p there will be more dollars demanded than at a rate of $1 = 50p. Hence we derive a normal, downward sloping demand curve for foreign currencies, as DD in Figure 5.9.

The supply of dollars in exchange for pounds comes, on the other hand, from British exporters who, having sold goods in the U.S.A., wish to convert the proceeds into the currency of their own country for spending. The supply comes also from such sources as American tourists in Britain and U.S. residents wishing to invest in the U.K.

11. For a proof of this proposition, see Katrak, *International Trade and the Balance of Payments*, Chapter 1.

For similar, but opposite, reasons to those advanced for the demand for dollars, the supply curve of dollars is likely to be upward sloping —the higher the price of dollars in terms of sterling (i.e. the more pence you get per dollar) the larger the quantity supplied.

When the supply and demand curves are put together as in Figure 5.9, we can easily identify the equilibrium exchange rate at which there are no dissatisfied buyers or sellers of pounds or dollars.

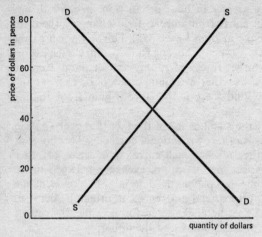

*Figure 5.9* Determination of the rate of exchange between pounds and dollars

Moreover, we can allow for changes of any kind, other than those due to an alteration of the exchange rate, which might affect supply or demand by, as usual, shifting the appropriate curve and observing the new equilibrium situation. For example, an increased desire by Americans to spend their holidays in Britain, or a decision by the U.S. Government to buy British anti-missile missiles, would shift the entire supply curve to the right. A belief that investment opportunities in the U.S.A. had improved, or a switch in tastes by pop fans from British to American groups would, on the other hand, shift the entire demand curve to the right.

## The balance of payments

Any country's international transactions may be recorded in what is known as its **Balance of Payments**, which is no more than an account of its dealings over a period of time with the rest of the world. The British Balance of Payments for a recent year is shown in simplified form in Table 5.2.

Table 5.2 **Balance of Payments, United Kingdom, 1969**

| *Current Account* | £ million | | £ million |
|---|---|---|---|
| Imports, visible | 7,202 | Exports, visible | 7,061 |
|      invisible | 3,572 |      invisible | 4,129 |
|     Total | 10,774 |     Total | 11,190 |
| Balance on Current Account | 416 | | |
| *Capital Account* | | | |
| Long-term private lending (by U.K.) | 617 | Long-term borrowing (by U.K.) | 684 |
| Official capital (net outflow) | 98 | | |
| Gold inflow | 44 | | |
| Short-term lending (net) | 341 | | |
|     Total | 1,100 |     Total | 684 |
| | | Balance on Capital Account | 416 |

Source: *United Kingdom Balance of Payments 1970* (H.M.S.O., 1970).

Exports and imports of goods (visible) and services (invisible) are entered in the **Current Account**, while flows of capital, both short term and long term, appear in the **Capital Account**, together with movements inwards or outwards of gold and foreign currency reserves.

The size of the items in a country's balance of payments is clearly related to the exchange rate between its own and foreign currencies. When foreign exchange is cheap, for example, the demand for imports will tend to be high. At the same time, our own pounds sterling will appear dear to foreigners, so that the demand for exports will tend to be low. If there is excess demand by the nationals of one country for the currency of others, pressure will be put on the foreign exchange rate and this will tend to make foreign currencies dearer in terms of our own. The balance of payments under such pressure is sometimes said to be in deficit.

As we might expect, one consequence of an excess demand for foreign currency, would be a rise in its price—i.e. a fall in the exchange rate. A movement of this kind might be self-equilibrating in the sense that supply and demand would become equal at a new, lower rate, leading to a restoration of equilibrium on the balance of payments.

The rising prices of imports, in terms of home currency, would normally check their expansion. Export prices, on the other hand, would tend to fall in terms of foreign prices as the rate of exchange declined, and one might therefore also expect the quantity of exports to expand as export prices fall to foreigners. However, the responsiveness (elasticity) of demand to changes in import and export prices may be small. The lower prices of exports may not lead to a sufficient increase in quantity to raise total receipts from exports. Similarly, the higher prices of imports would not lead to much reduction in their quantity if demand was highly inelastic. Furthermore, on the Capital Account, there may be a tendency for speculative demands for foreign exchange to increase, simply because speculators expect, and hope for, a still further fall in the exchange rate.

If it is considered unlikely that a deterioration in the exchange rate will bring about an equality of supply and demand, then one must face the fact that the exchange rate may tend to move still further against the home currency. Such a continuing **devaluation** in the external purchasing power of a country's currency means that the quantity of imports that can be bought with a fixed amount of exports is falling. Not surprisingly, this situation is generally considered undesirable.

For this reason governments often intervene in the market for foreign exchange, and a number of international institutions have been created to try to reduce fluctuations in the values of national currencies. The main method used by a government is simply to enter the foreign exchange market as a potential buyer or seller. The state must first provide itself with a quantity of domestic and of foreign currencies. Then, according to whether the exchange rate is tending to move against or in favour of their own currency, they offer for sale, or demand to buy, foreign exchange, so as to keep equality between total supply and demand.

The extent to which a policy of intervention in the foreign exchange market can be successfully maintained is limited by the size of the currency reserves in the hands of the nation. In the face of persistent heavy excess demand for foreign exchange, the stock of foreign currency may well be too small to prevent the price being bid up. In such circumstances the alternatives facing a country can include the following:

i. Allow devaluation to take place naturally.
ii. Impose tariffs and other duties on imports, and restrictions (exchange control) on the purchase of foreign currencies for other purposes (travel, investment, etc.), thereby reducing the demand for foreign exchange.
iii. Obtain loans from other governments or from international agencies, in the hope that the passage of time will bring a relief of pressure.

It will be realised that the more successful one country is in improving its balance of payments, the more likely it is to cause difficulties for the rest of the world, and provoke retaliation by other countries. Competitive devaluations and retaliatory impositions of import controls tend, therefore, to be regarded as undesirable, because they may be self-defeating and at the same time limit the scope of world trade. A country in balance of payments difficulties is, therefore, often encouraged to try to avoid the need for restrictive action of these kinds by getting to the root cause of its troubles. Its problem may, for example, stem from too rapid a rate of internal price inflation, leading to a gradual reduction in the competitiveness of its exports. Alternatively, it can be the result of too rapid a rate of growth of domestic incomes, leading to an excessive demand for imports.

Rapid inflation and economic growth might both yield to alternative economic policies. Restrictive monetary controls, which we discussed in the previous section, might, for instance, be used to force interest rates up and prices down. We should, however, be careful to consider all the side effects of such a policy, which might be successful from the point of view of the balance of payments only at the expense of other economic goals, including the maintenance of full employment. We consider policy conflicts of this kind in Chapter 8.

# Chapter 6

# National Income and Expenditure

We began this book with a puzzle about variations in family expenditure on housing. It led us to consider how resources are allocated in a market economy. The time has now come to concentrate attention on the size of the total *national income*.

The branch of economics which deals with aggregates, of which the national income is the most important, is known as **macroeconomics**.[1] Here we view the economy as a whole and ignore the detailed pattern of resource allocation between individual sectors. Prices and production are still our concern, but they are the average *general* price level, and the volume of *total* output.

This new macroeconomic viewpoint will give us a chance to view the economy from a different perspective. There is a small price to be paid for this, however. The tools of analysis which we have learnt so far will no longer do all the jobs that are required. We shall, therefore, have to develop some slightly different ones. We need them because we want eventually to examine what determines the national income. Hence, we might do worse than ask exactly what that phrase really means.

### The circular flow of income and expenditure in a two-sector economy

We may, for once, start with a definition. The **national income**, or **national product**, is a measure of the total value of goods and services produced by a country in a given period of time. It is both a measure of output and of the income of the factors of production. The identical nature of these magnitudes can be demonstrated with the help of a diagram, which emphasises the circular nature of the flows of income and expenditure.

Suppose we have a simple isolated economy, in which there is no government activity, and in which there are only two sectors, a business sector and a household sector. We further assume that businesses do all the producing of consumer goods, which they sell to house-

1. In contrast to **microeconomics,** which deals with questions of resource allocation.

holds; while the latter own all the factors of production which they sell to businesses for the purpose of producing the national output of goods and services.

Figure 6.1 shows the circular flow of income, expenditure, and output for this two sector economy. Consider, first, the lower portion of the diagram. Business output is shown as flowing to households in return for household expenditure. That is to say, the spending of

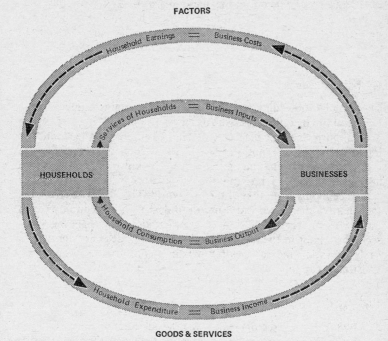

FACTORS

GOODS & SERVICES

*Figure 6.1* The circular flow of expenditure and income

money by households that flows to businesses in exchange for goods and services—the money value of total business output—*is* the amount of total expenditure on it. But this expenditure by households can be viewed also as providing business with its income. Hence, total expenditure is the same as the value of output, and the same as total business income. All three are only different ways of looking at the same flow of money payments.

The upper portion of Figure 6.1 illustrates the counterpart flows of the services of the factors of production and payments for these services. The arrows starting in the household sector represent the money value of the flows of the services of these factors, as members of households work for businesses in return for wages, and provide capital in return for interest, etc. These two flows are equal because total spending by businesses on factor services (i.e. their total costs) *is the same* as the total receipts (or earnings) of households for providing these services. Moreover, since total business income accrues to households as factor payments, the money value of flows in the upper and lower portions of the diagram are also equal to each other. That is to say, the value of total output is the same as total expenditure, which is the same as total factor incomes derived from the process of production.[2]

## Oversimplifications

The circular flow diagram just described, contains a great many highly simplified features which, nevertheless, do not affect the general purpose of the diagram, which is to emphasise the identity of income, expenditure, and product flows. Before looking at the size and trends of national income in the U.K., however, we must take a brief look at two important complications which separate our simple economy from that of the real world. The first arises from the fact that we shall later find it useful to deal with an economy which has two sectors in addition to households and businesses. The second pertains to the fact that national output does not consist entirely of goods and services for personal consumption. Some part consists of capital.

## Circular flow in a four-sector economy

The two additional sectors which we now add to our simple economy comprise the government and the rest of the world. They appear in a slightly more complicated diagram, Figure 6.2, which is otherwise of the same general form as Figure 6.1.

i. *Government*. The state enters the picture in two main ways. In the first place, the government purchases certain goods and services, such as guns and crime protection, for itself. In the second place, the state acts as tax gatherer and disburser of **transfer** payments to supple-

---

2. We treat profit as a factor reward accruing to the factor of production enterprise. There is, therefore, no residual 'profit' remaining in the business sector. All business income is passed on to households, who own all factors of production.

ment the incomes of private individuals and others. The chief of these flows of income and expenditure are shown in the upper portion of Figure 6.2.

Taxes are levied on households (e.g. personal income taxes) and on businesses (e.g. corporation tax), and these appear as flows from the two private sectors to the government. Transfer payments, on the

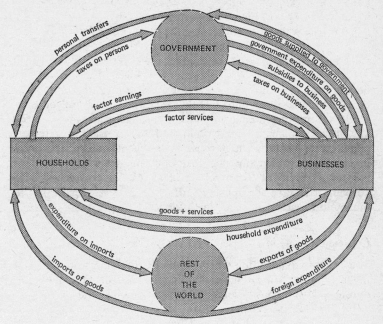

*Figure 6.2* Circular flow in an open economy with a government sector

other hand, are shown as flows from the government; they are also made both to households (e.g. retirement pensions and unemployment benefits) and to businesses (e.g. subsidies to industries which the government wishes to support, and to firms which agree to locate factories in areas which the authorities favour). In Britain, something like two-fifths of all expenditure is channelled through central and local governments. Hence it is obviously vital to take account of the influence of the state if we are to be able to relate our argument to the real world.

ii. *The rest of the world.* The need to take account of the rest of the world in describing the circular flows of income and expenditure is due to the fact that most countries today are not self-sufficient economically, but engage in trade with foreigners. For the United Kingdom, this matter is of immense importance. As has already been said, between a fifth and a quarter of all income and expenditure flows are attributable to international transactions of one sort or another.

The major kinds of international payments and receipts are for imports and exports. Figure 6.2 portrays them in the lower portion of the diagram, where a sector termed the 'Rest of the World' is shown. The fact that some of the outputs of (British) businesses supply consumers elsewhere, emphasises the fact that overseas countries exercise an influence on the British economy, affecting the size of business income in Britain and, therefore, the level of the national income. At the same time, the fact that the British purchase goods and services from foreign countries shows that their economies are equally open to influence from Britain's. Moreover, the last statements remain true, whatever the purposes of payments and receipts across international frontiers may be. It does not matter whether money is paid or received for the purchase of goods, for enjoying holidays abroad, or to take advantage of attractive interest rates for lending money to foreign persons or institutions.

### Consumption and investment

The second complication which limits the usefulness of our simple model of an economy to understanding the real world is that national output does not consist solely of consumer goods and services, but also of capital equipment.

We are already familiar, from Chapter 2, with the idea of capital as a separate factor of production. Capital includes outputs of goods, such as machinery, factory buildings, and equipment which, in contrast to consumer goods, are not wanted by households for their own sake but are used by businesses to aid production. Capital goods are necessary for modern processes of production, and may be viewed as *indirectly* helping businesses to produce consumer goods more efficiently. Indeed, one reason why we are so much more efficient as a nation than we were a hundred or so years ago is that we have accumulated such a large amount of capital goods of various kinds. For this reason, most advanced economies currently devote some 10 to 20 per cent of their resources to the production of capital goods.

Additions to a nation's stock of capital during a period is called **investment**. We shall find it extremely useful to distinguish between expenditure on consumption and that on investment. The principle for distinguishing between them is fairly straightforward, but when we come to apply the distinction to particular items we are at times faced with some tricky problems. These need not bother us unduly, but we must be prepared to find that capital is sometimes used in a sense which we might not expect. For instance, consumption implies the satisfaction of a want directly by consumers, and the 'using up' or even the 'destruction' of goods in the actual process of consumption—e.g., when we eat an egg, tip detergent into the washing machine, or burn petrol as we drive a car. Some consumer goods, however, such as cars and houses, provide a service over a long period of time. Durable goods of this kind represent, in a sense, capital, because they are not used up immediately but are available for future consumption without further production. We shall sometimes find it useful to include such outputs as part of the nation's investment.

Finally, there is one special case to be considered. By convention, economists include changes in the value of **stocks** of goods and materials as part of investment. Stocks (inventories in American terminology) consist of output in the pipeline, as it were, between production and consumption. They include, on the one hand, raw materials and, on the other, semi-manufactured and unsold consumer goods. The former are classed as 'working capital' to distinguish them from 'fixed capital', such as plant and machinery. The latter are 'almost' part of consumption, but are not really so until they are actually bought by consumers.

The size of the nation's stocks is part of the national capital existing at a point in time. Provided there is no change in the value of stocks between the beginning and the end of the period over which we wish to estimate the national income, there is no reason to take account of them. If, however, there is a *change* in the value of stocks, the situation is quite different. For instance, if the value of stocks increases during the period, this amounts to an increase in capital, and therefore should be treated as investment. Likewise and for the same reason, a decrease in the value of stocks is considered negative investment.

### The national income of the United Kingdom

We may now refer to official statistics to find that the national income of the United Kingdom in 1969 amounted to about £35,000 million. We know that this means that all the goods and services produced in that year, valued at their (current) prices, were worth £35,000 million or approaching £700 per man, woman, and child in the population. However quickly the publisher gets this book into your hands, it is quite certain that the figures will now be out of date. You should therefore make a point of looking up for yourself what the national income was estimated to have been for the latest years you can find.[3] Work out, too, how much it has increased in

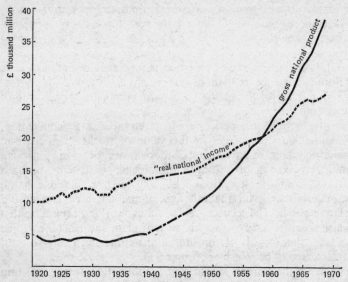

*Figure 6.3* Gross National Product at factor cost at current price and Gross (Real) National Income at constant prices since 1921

percentage terms since 1969. It will bring home to you that it is very much more interesting to watch what happens to the national income as time passes, than to pay great attention to its value in any particular year.

Figure 6.3. has been prepared to show the trend in the national income over the fifty years since the end of the First World War. There are two lines on this graph. Concentrate first on the unbroken line, and ignore the war years. The line is labelled gross national product. The exact meaning of this expression will be described shortly, but we may accept it now as being a measure of all the

3. Try the *Annual Abstract of Statistics, National Income and Expenditure,* or *Economic Trends,* all published by H.M.S.O. for the Central Statistical Office.

goods and services produced each year, valued at the prices ruling at the time.

What are the most important characteristics of this historical series that we can observe from the graph? If we ask this question immediately, we can see in advance what kind of economic theories we are going to be interested in. The graph has two main features:

i. It slopes generally upwards.
ii. It is not a smooth curve.

Let us examine each of these characteristics, for they conveniently introduce the main branches of macroeconomic theory, economic growth, inflation, and the trade cycle.

### Why has the national income risen since 1920?

As you can see from the graph, the national income grew about sevenfold in the fifty year span since the First World War. There are two distinct reasons why this could have taken place. The first is the straightforward one that the physical quantities of goods and services rose. There is no doubt that this is part of the explanation. Production has increased in Britain, as it has in other countries. Economists discuss the causes in their theories of growth, which remains one of the most difficult areas of economics, and we shall not be able to say much about it in this introductory book.

There is, however, a second important explanation for the rising value of the national income in the statistics. If, between two years, the money value of the outputs of goods and services increase without any growth in their quantities, then the explanation must be that the prices at which the goods are measured have risen. As everyone knows, we live in an age of rising prices (or **inflation**) and a second area of macroeconomics is concerned with the analysis of the causes of inflation.

Inflation may be measured by calculating the rise in the *average* level of prices from year to year. Figures are collected of the prices of a representative collection of goods and services bought by households in Britain. The percentage change in each item is given a bias (or 'weight') corresponding to its importance in household expenditure. The average price change, so calculated, is representative of the changing cost of living, and is not unduly influenced by very large price changes in minor items.[4] Statistics measuring average price

4. Such an average is called weighted, to distinguish it from a straightforward average. An example may be helpful. Suppose there are two items in the family

movements are generally in the form of **index numbers**. They are constructed by taking one year, which is called the base, and referring

Table 6.1    **Price index numbers of all goods and services sold on the U.K. market**

| Year | (*Year 1963 = 100*)<br>*Price index number* |
| --- | --- |
| 1958 | 100·0 |
| 1959 | 101·2 |
| 1960 | 102·8 |
| 1961 | 105·9 |
| 1962 | 109·8 |
| 1963 | 112·2 |
| 1964 | 115·9 |
| 1965 | 121·4 |
| 1966 | 126·4 |
| 1967 | 130·0 |
| 1968 | 135·9 |
| 1969 | 142·9 |

Source: *National Income and Expenditure 1970* (H.M.S.O.)

to the average price level in that base year as 100. The price index number for another year is then expressed as a percentage of that of

budget—food, the price of which doubled over the period; and clothing, the price of which rose threefold. Hence, the price index of food alone is 200 on the base year of 100, while for clothing it is 300. To start with, assume that food and clothing have equal weights. We would then get the same result if we took 0·5 of the price index for each item multiplying each price index by its own weight.

|  | *Weight* | | *Price Index* (last year = 100) | |
| --- | --- | --- | --- | --- |
| Food | 0·5 | × | 200 | = 100 |
| Clothing | 0·5 | × | 300 | = 150 |
| All | 1·0 | | Average | = 250 |

But suppose now food was four times as important in the family budget as clothing. Weights would be 0·8 for food, and 0·2 for clothing, and the weighted average price index would be only 220.

| Food | 0·8 | × | 200 | = 160 |
| --- | --- | --- | --- | --- |
| Clothing | 0·2 | × | 300 | = 60 |
| All | 1·0 | | Average | = 220 |

The rise is, of course, smaller because the price of food, the item with the larger weight, has risen less than the price of clothing.

the base. So in Table 6.1 it can be seen that prices rose 1·2 per cent from 1958 to 1959, and 42·9 per cent from 1958 to 1969.

Let us now turn back to Figure 6.3. In order to make an assessment of the extent to which the increase in national income between 1921 and 1969 was attributable to the rise in prices, we make use of a series of price index numbers. Over so long a period as fifty years, we should not regard such an index as having a very precise meaning. The physical goods in the shops were not the same at the end of the period as they were at the beginning, so that we have to approximate for price changes where old goods disappear and new ones take their place (e.g. electric blankets instead of stone hot water bottles). But defects of detail can be overlooked if our need is only for broad magnitudes.

In Figure 6.3, we have used a price index to **deflate** values calculated at current prices to produce what is known as **real** income—i.e. income adjusted for price changes. The unbroken line on the graph shows the course of real income over the same period as that of the broken line which represents money income. Real income, calculated for each year in terms of constant prices, rose between two and threefold since 1921, compared with the sevenfold rise in money income. In other words, prices must have nearly trebled over the period.[5]

## Why has the national income not risen at a steady rate?

Let us turn to the second question raised about Figure 6.3. Close inspection shows that, although real income exhibits a persistent upward trend, it does so at a variable rather than at a steady rate. Figure 6.4 brings this out more clearly by plotting the year to year *changes* in income. While in some years the national income grew in real terms by as much as 5 per cent, in others it hardly grew at all, and in a few years it actually declined. But picking on individual years tells only half the story. The other half is that good and bad years do not appear at random, but tend to come in runs. More precisely, there is a history of **cycles** in the trend of income and output. There are periods of boom when income rises fairly steadily;

5. It is worth avoiding a common error. If output and prices each rise by 10 per cent, national income at current prices rises by 21 per cent not 20 per cent, since value equals price *times* quantity, i.e. 110 per cent of 110 per cent is 121 per cent. So also, if output is two and a half times, and money national income is seven times that of the base year then the imputed price rise is 700 per cent divided by 250 per cent = 280 per cent. This is *very* roughly what has happened in the fifty years since the First World War ended.

then a crisis followed by a slump, in which output drops to a low level from which it may fail to recover for some time.

This cyclical behaviour is termed by economists the **trade**, or **business, cycle**. It was characteristic of the British economy in the nineteenth and early twentieth centuries, though cycles of quite a different duration have been noted. Since the end of the Second

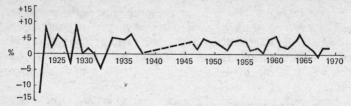

*Figure 6.4* Year-to-year changes in national income since 1921 (per cent)

World War, such cycles have very greatly diminished in intensity. One reason may be that economists now understand better the forces creating the cycles, and governments can more easily control them; but there has been a complete change in the social climate which has probably helped too. Hence the period since 1945 shows the behaviour of the economy which has been influenced by government policy directed at reducing the swings of the trade cycle. The graph, however, goes back to the 1920s, and the classic cyclical period, in the 1920s and '30s can be clearly seen—three or four boom years, followed by a crisis and slump and recovery in the mid-thirties. This particular cycle was, typically, not confined to Britain, but affected virtually every country in the world. Moreover, the crisis was so catastrophic, and the slump so severe and prolonged, that it has come to be known as the Great Depression.

Britain suffered rather less of a decline after the world crash of 1931 than did many other countries, including the U.S.A. The reason, however, was largely that we, in this country, had not experienced so sharp a boom to take us to such great heights from which to tumble. But the depression was real enough to two and a half million jobless workers, about 20 per cent of the total labour force. Even higher unemployment rates, topping the 40 per cent mark, persisted in certain industries like shipbuilding, coal, and steel, with dramatic effects because of the heavy concentration of these industries in certain areas such as South Wales, Scotland, and the North of England, which were known as depressed areas because of the disastrous effect of the slump on their economies.

It is not surprising that economists began to turn their attention to analysing the causes of the world wide economic depression, which dazed everyone with its severity. Outstanding among those who contributed to the understanding of the problem was John Maynard Keynes. His *General Theory of Employment, Interest and Money*, published in 1936, has probably been the most influential book by an economist in the present century. Most of the new tools we mentioned at the beginning of the chapter that we should need found their first expression here, and it is to them that we shall shortly turn.

## *How well does the national income measure the standard of living?*

We have first one preliminary task. The implication has been drawn above that, since the national income is a measure of the value of goods and services produced, it is an indicator also of living standards. This is, of course, not untrue. We write deliberately in the double negative to give pause for thought. The national income is one indicator of living standards, but the two are not the same thing.

### The national accounts

There are several reasons why we should be careful about assuming that a rise in real national income means also an equivalent rise in living standards for the population.

i. *The population may have changed.* In Britain, the total number of persons alive has been rising on average by something over $\frac{1}{2}$ per cent per annum over recent years. So our post-war growth rate of real national income of about $2\frac{1}{2}$ per cent per annum is approximately 2 per cent if calculated per head of the population.

ii. *Exclusions.* The National Income does not measure *everything* that makes up the community's living standards. In the first place, there are completely non-economic matters, like the weather. Other things being equal, it is cheaper to live in a warm, temperate climate than one with very cold winters. You need less clothing and fuel, so there is more to spare for other things. Similarly, the statistics do not take full account of undesirable features of life like noises and air pollution.

There are also technical reasons why the national income cannot efficiently measure everything that affects living standards. One is that only *marketed* goods and services are included, because of the difficulty of counting and pricing such items as home-made radio sets and the services of housewives, for example.[6] If every man stopped do-it-youself jobs around the house, divorced his wife, and employed her as a housekeeper, the national income might rise without anyone being significantly better off. It is doubtful whether making allowance for non-marketed services would significantly affect the growth rate for Britain. But it may be worth while casting a critical eye on this count at growth rates for less developed countries. Economic development is usually accompanied by a switch from subsistence living within the family to growing reliance on specialisation and the exchange of goods and services in the market. Hence, if the market sector only were included in the calculation of national income, the recorded growth rate would be exaggerated.

Another exclusion from the measured national income is the quality dimension of the goods and services produced. Statisticians try to make some allowance for quality changes, but it is virtually impossible to do so with much accuracy. How much 'better' is today's car than that of 20 or 30 years ago? It is certainly a very different article. Some people even claim that quality has deteriorated, because comfort has been sacrificed for performance. But even if there are no contrary judgments, the problem persists. Take this book, for example. If you open it flat every time you turn the page you should not do any damage to the spine (so the publishers claim). But if you had done the same thing to an early paperback, you would have completely broken the back.

The final exclusion from the national income as conventionally measured is probably the most important of all—leisure. The average hours worked in manufacturing industry in Britain has dropped slightly but significantly by one or two hours per week in the last ten years. If we assume that people value extra leisure at, say, the (opportunity cost) rate of wages they sacrificed, we could even make a shot at valuing this contribution to higher living standards. But the fact remains that no account is taken of leisure in the national income calculations.

iii. *Capital and income*. The third reason for distinguishing between the national income and the standard of living is that the former values *all* goods and services produced, including capital items like

6. This is not strictly true for all such products. Services provided free by the state are included in the national income. So, for example, is the value of food produced and consumed on farms.

machines and factories, while the standard of living is related more closely to expenditure on consumption goods. In so far as the nation is adding to, or using up, its stock of wealth, therefore, the standard of living can lag behind, or advance ahead of, changes in the national income.

Allowance for all capital expenditure should be made before commenting on living standards in any particular year. Interestingly enough, some account of part of the expenditure by the nation on capital goods is also made in the national accounts. The reason is as follows. The nation has a stock of capital, which helps to produce goods and services efficiently. As time passes these producer's goods wear out and become obsolete or, in jargon, **depreciate**. Unless this depreciation is made good by putting aside enough resources to replace worn out, obsolete equipment, the stock of capital must fall. We, therefore, find that a depreciation allowance is deducted from the calculated **gross national product (G.N.P.)** to give a new figure known as the **net national product (N.N.P.)**—i.e. G.N.P. minus depreciation = N.N.P. Estimating the amount of depreciation (or **capital consumption**, to use the official statisticians' term) that is occurring is, inevitably, a somewhat arbitrary business, which involves predicting the future. Unless you know in advance whether a machine will last 3 or 5 years, for example (physically, or before it is rendered obsolete), you do not know how to estimate what part of its value you should count as having depreciated during the first year of its life.

We cannot go further into this important question here. But it is useful to know that capital consumption is estimated to have absorbed approximately 10 per cent of the gross national product per annum in the U.K. over recent years. We should interpret the figure of net national product, after deduction of depreciation, as the value of goods and services which is available for all purposes in the economy—after, that is, allowance has been made for maintaining the value of the nation's capital stock more or less intact.

iv. *The distribution of income.* Last on our list of cautions about taking the national income as an indicator of living standards is the question of income distribution. Two points need to be made. First, and most simply, a change in total income need not imply that *everyone*'s income has risen by the same amount. We must remember that we are looking only at averages and that some incomes may even fall when the average is rising.

The second point is slightly more subtle. When we were discussing the difference between real and money income, we talked of using a price index for deflating money values expressed in current prices. But we could, in reality, use any of a number of different price indices, each of which might give quite a different average of identical price changes. The reason is associated with the weights which, you may remember (see footnote, p. 107), are supposed to be representative of the relative importance of each item in total expenditure. Which weights are to be used?

For the national income we may take total expenditure on each item in the economy. But for any individual consumer the appropriate weights would be those representing the relative importance of each good in his own budget. This may depend on many things: his tastes, the region where he lives, his family circumstances, etc. Of particular importance in determining expenditure patterns, as we saw in Chapter 1, is a household's income. If you turn back to Table 1.2 on page 11, you will see again that, for example, food expenditure tends to fall in proportion to total expenditure as income rises, while expenditure on clothing increases. If, for example, the price of food were to rise by 10 per cent while the price of clothing rose by only 5 per cent, we might expect, other things being equal, that living standards would fall relatively more sharply for the poor than for the rich.

### Government

Our discussion of the national accounts has so far been based upon the assumption that we are dealing with a closed economy which neither engages in international transactions with other countries nor has a government. The world is not, of course, like this. We must, therefore, consider some of the implications of being more realistic.

The introduction of a government sector has two important implications for the national accounts.

i. *Disposable income.* The government imposes taxes on the *incomes* of individuals and thereby reduces the sum available for free spending. The practice is, therefore, adopted of making separate estimates of personal factor incomes after the deduction of direct taxes. If additions are also made for any direct transfers of income to persons (e.g. retirement pensions), the resulting total is called **disposable** (personal) income. Disposable income represents the sum available to the individual, which he can decide to spend (or save) as he pleases.

ii. *Factor cost versus market prices*. If a tax is placed on a *commodity*, a gap is created between the cost of producing it, represented by the amount paid to all the factors of production, and the price at which it is sold in the market. Two alternative valuations of the national output are therefore available, and the national statisticians use both when they prepare the national accounts. One is the national product at **factor cost**, the other at **market prices**. The difference between the two is accounted for by taxes on expenditure (*net* of any subsidies). Thus, G.N.P. at factor cost *plus* taxes (*minus* subsidies) on goods and services = G.N.P. at market prices. Each measure has its uses. In the British national accounts the term G.N.P. is often used without further specification to mean G.N.P. at factor cost.

### The rest of the world

International transactions must be briefly discussed because income in Britain does not all originate within the country. If Britain were a self-sufficient, closed economy, we could simply equate **domestic** product with *national* product. Fortunately, however, the adjustment needed here is relatively straightforward. We add to domestic product the net income received from abroad.

### How the different national aggregates fit together

We have dealt in some detail with the technicalities of the preparation of the national accounts. It may help to place the main aggregates in their correct perspective if we try to build them up with a numerical example for a very simple economy.

Suppose, once more, we have a country where there are only two producing sectors, agriculture and industry, and only one consuming sector, households. We make the further assumption that industry sells all its products to households. Agriculture, on the other hand, produces food for sale to households, but also wool for sale to industry for making into clothing. Set out below in Table 6.2 are all the receipts and payments made in each producing sector of the country, which we shall call Bisectoria, for the year ending 31 December 1999.

We assume complete absence of government and no foreign transactions, so as to obtain an economy which resembles closely that described earlier in this chapter. In that economy we saw that the total expenditure on goods and services is only another way of

Table 6.2   **Income and expenditure of agriculture and industry for the economy of Bisectoria for the year ending 31 December 1999**

| Agriculture | | | | Industry | | | |
|---|---|---|---|---|---|---|---|
| Payments | $ | Receipts | $ | Payments | $ | Receipts | $ |
| Wages and Profits | 500 | Sales to industry | 100 | Wages and profits | 900 | Sales to households | 1,000 |
| | | Sales to households | 400 | Purchases from agriculture | 100 | | |
| | 500 | | 500 | | 1,000 | | 1,000 |

looking at the total receipts by businesses for their sales, and that total costs of producing these goods are only the reverse side of a coin representing total incomes of the factors of production. It follows that we can calculate the national income for the whole of Bisectoria in at least three ways:

   i. Total factor incomes.
   ii. Total expenditure.
   iii. Total production.

and we can derive (i) and (ii) at the same time by constructing an account to list all the payments and receipts of households in 1999, as in Table 6.3.

Table 6.3   **Income and expenditure of households for the economy of Bisectoria for the year ending 31 December 1999**

| Payments | $ | Receipts | $ |
|---|---|---|---|
| Purchases from agriculture | 400 | Wages and profits in agriculture | 500 |
| Purchases from industry | 1,000 | Wages and profits in industry | 900 |
| | 1,400 | | 1,400 |

   i. National income in Bisectoria is the sum of all factor incomes, or the total of the right hand column in Table 6.3, $1,400.
   ii. National expenditure in Bisectoria is the sum of all purchases of goods and services, or the total of the left-hand column in Table 6.3, $1,400.

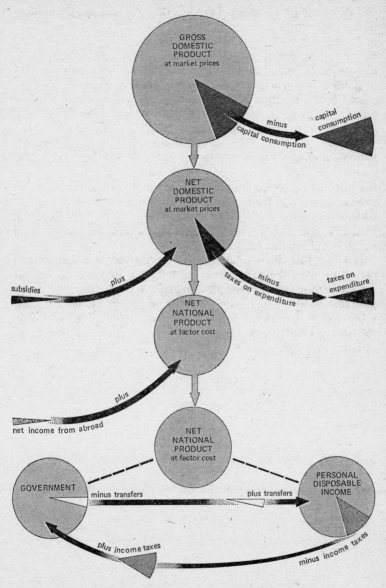

GROSS
DOMESTIC
PRODUCT
at market prices

minus
capital consumption

capital
consumption

NET
DOMESTIC
PRODUCT
at market prices

subsidies

plus

minus
taxes on expenditure

taxes on
expenditure

NET
NATIONAL
PRODUCT
at factor cost

plus

net income from abroad

NET
NATIONAL
PRODUCT
at factor cost

GOVERNMENT

minus transfers

plus transfers

PERSONAL
DISPOSABLE
INCOME

plus income taxes

minus income taxes

*Figure 6.5* The national accounts; relationships between the main aggregates

To obtain the total national product (iii), we must add the production of agriculture and of industry in Table 6.2. First, agriculture produced goods worth $500. Second, industry—but we must be rather careful here. If we were to count the total sales to households of $1,000, we should be making a mistake. For a part of the sales of industry are articles of clothing, and for the production of these wool was bought from agriculture. So if we were to include all the output of agriculture ($500) *and* all the output of industry ($1,000), we would be counting the production of wool twice.

In order to avoid such **double counting** when calculating the national output, we must include only what is called the **value added** by each industry. Value added is defined as the value of output *less* the cost of output (really input) of raw materials, and semi-finished products bought in from other firms. In Bisectoria, industrial value added is $1,000 *minus* $100 of purchases from agriculture (i.e. $900). National product is therefore $500 of agricultural output plus $900 of industrial production, namely $1,400.

It would be tedious to complicate the Bisectorial economy with details to allow the computation of different numerical values for every one of the other national aggregates. We therefore simply suppose that we have a total gross domestic product of $1,400 and show schematically, in Figure 6.5, how the others would be derived. All the relationships have been discussed before, so there is no need to go into them further.

# Chapter 7

# Income Determination

The last chapter was concerned with the meaning of the national income and with problems in estimating its value over a period of time. We did not ask the question why the national income had reached its particular level. It is our purpose now to answer this important question—to see how the national income is determined.

### Flows of income and expenditure, *ex ante* and *ex post*

In order to understand the nature of the forces which determine income at the macroeconomic level we must first appreciate that there are two entirely different ways of looking at economic events. So far, we have been looking at the national income in a way which is, in a sense, historical.

We have always taken as a datum that the events have taken place; the year is over and past; expenditure has been made; output has been created; goods have been produced; incomes have been earned. This way of looking at things after they have occurred is dubbed **realised** or *ex post*. To put it differently, we observed what *actually* was achieved.

In contrast, there is another way of looking at the same economic phenomena. We can interest ourselves in expenditure *before* it occurs. In so doing, we shall be able to consider *determinants* of behaviour. So, when we discuss **planned** or *ex ante* expenditure (as it is called), we are concerned with the amounts that people *plan*, *desire*, or *intend* to spend on goods and services rather than what was realised (*ex post*) in the past.

As a matter of fact, we used these concepts implicitly earlier in the book when we were discussing the formation of market price, though we did not use this terminology. What we called demand curves are no more than *ex ante* statements of the amounts that consumers wish or plan to buy of a product at a range of prices. Supply curves, similarly, are statements of the *planned* quantities that would be offered for sale over the same price range. The realised (*ex post*) quantities, on the other hand, are the amounts actually bought and sold. The latter are only the same as the (*ex ante*) planned quantities if market price happens to be at equilibrium.

Suppose market price is not at but below equilibrium.[1] We know this means that in such conditions demand will exceed supply. Now, however, we can appreciate that this is true only in the *ex ante* sense— i.e. the quantity that consumers plan to buy at the market price is greater than the quantity that sellers plan to sell. It is not true in the *ex post*, realised sense, because the quantity of goods actually sold must inevitably be the same as the quantity actually bought.

When we look back at what happened in the market, *ex post*, we see only this equality of realised magnitudes, and not the frustrated plans of buyers and/or sellers. Since, however, the plans or desires of consumers and producers do *not* coincide, we know that the market is not in equilibrium, and that the forces of demand and supply will normally operate to change price.

In contrast, consider the situation in equilibrium. The amount consumers plan to buy matches that which sellers plan to offer for sale; planned (*ex ante*) demand equals planned (*ex ante*) supply, and there is no pressure on market price. Our definition of equilibrium turns out to be: where planned *ex ante* demand and supply are equal.

Let us now transfer our new-found terminology from the realm of the individual market place, where prices act as an equilibrating force, to macroeconomics. Here, as we shall see, changes in the level of the national income can take on the role of bringing about equality in the plans of the whole community.

Let us deal with this question of the determination of the national income in the simplest possible economy, one in which the only expenditure is on consumer goods; where there are only two sectors, households and businesses; and where there is no change in the general price level, so that the national income is measured in real terms. This economy is in fact similar to the one with which we became familiar in Chapter 6, which was represented diagrammatically in Figure 6.1, page 101. The most important observation we made there about that economy, which is now of the utmost relevance, was that total income was equal to total expenditure. We can now go further and say that the income was generated by the expenditure on goods and services. It was because people bought goods and services that the factors of production derived their income from the proceeds. Expenditure, in a sense, created income.

1. We assume also that the supply and demand curves slope up and down respectively.

## Equilibrium income

This treatment involved an *ex post* way of looking at what actually did happen, and we cannot therefore tell whether planned expenditure matched incomes or not. Look at it from the *ex ante* point of view. Suppose that people had really planned (*ex ante*) to spend, during the current period of a year, exactly all of their original income that they received in the previous year. In that case, planned expenditure precisely matched previous, original (*ex post*) income. *Hence income must have been at an equilibrium level.* And by equilibrium we mean no more than the absence of economic forces to bring any pressure on the level of income to change.

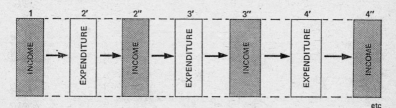

etc

*Figure 7.1* Income and expenditure flows in equilibrium

Schematically, we have the kind of situation shown in Figure 7.1. Start at position 1 with a level of income equal to the size of the rectangle below the number, and determined by previous expenditure of the same amount. Now assume that people plan to spend all of their income, neither more nor less, indicated by the box 2′. If they do so, the result will be that income generated by the expenditure 2″ will be equal to original (*ex post*) income 1. There is no force tending to increase or lower it, and no reason why income should change in periods 2, 3, or 4.

Now suppose, instead, that the community wanted to spend less than its income, as depicted in Figure 7.2. As before, we start with

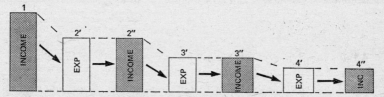

*Figure 7.2* Income and expenditure flows in disequilibrium. Falling income

generated (*ex post*) income equal to the size of the box under the number 1. Now planned expenditure is less than the original (*ex post*) income. Box 2′ is smaller than box 1. Again if plans are realised, the amount of income generated (2″) will also be smaller than the original income 1. Income is not in equilibrium, it is falling and will continue to do so because, in the diagram, consumers never plan to spend all of their income. Note, incidentally than even when income is not in equilibrium, looking back (*ex post*) realised income is, nevertheless, equal to realised expenditure. When the year is over, the statisticians will measure income and find that it was not the size of rectangle 1, but was the same as expenditure, because 2′ = 2″.

Figure 7.3 is reproduced for symmetry. It shows how planned expenditure greater than income tends to cause income to rise. There

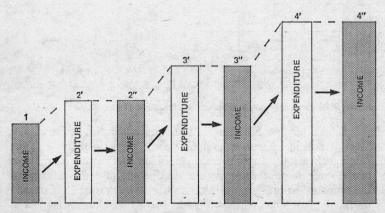

*Figure 7.3* Income and expenditure flows in disequilibrium. Rising income

should be no need to explain it. We should, perhaps, mention only that planned expenditure greater than income is perfectly feasible, provided one has past savings to draw upon, or can obtain credit from a shop-keeper, a bank, or from some other quarter.

### Income determination

All this may be very well, the reader may argue, but we have not yet said anything about the level at which income will settle. What we have done is only to suggest that income will be at an equilibrium level when the community's total spending plans exactly match its previous income. We need now some information about what determines expenditure. We need an **expenditure function,** i.e. a statement which describes exactly what expenditure plans depend upon.

We should emphasise that the simple model of an economy with which we are dealing has only one type of expenditure, that on consumption. This is obviously unrealistic. We shall find, however, that this simplification will help accustom us to a new tool of economic analysis, and we shall drop the assumption shortly. One reason why it is helpful to concentrate first upon consumption expenditure alone is that consumption is known to be closely related to income itself. Although there are several other determinants of total consumption expenditure, we may, in the short run, neglect them by making an assumption that all these other things are unchanging. Consumption is left simply as a function of income, though we may add the hypothesis that consumption is an *increasing* function of income, i.e. that the association between them is positive. When income rises so does consumption, and vice versa.

### Aggregate demand

Look now at the graph Figure 7.4, and let us sometimes cut short our sentences by using letters to stand for words that we need to use often, as follows:

$Y$ stands for Income[2]
$E$ stands for Expenditure
$C$ stands for Consumption

On the horizontal axis of the graph we measure income. On the vertical axis we measure expenditure. We also use the same scale for the two axes.

Let us first construct a curve of planned total expenditure or **aggregate demand.** We have assumed that the sole constituent element of expenditure is consumption, which is solely dependent on income. We therefore draw the line $EE$ to represent the community's planned consumption spending at every level of income. $EE$ slopes upwards because we also assumed that consumption was an increasing function of income. Thus if income has a numerical value represented by the horizontal distance $OB$ (i.e. if $Y = OB$), planned consumption $= BG$. If $Y = OA$, planned $C = AZ$, and so forth. The curve $EE$ is known as the aggregate demand curve, because it

2. $Y$ is the conventional symbol for aggregate income. $I$ stands for another magnitude, as we shall shortly see.

represents the total demand of the community in money terms; i.e. its total planned expenditure at different levels of income.

Next let us inspect the line *ON*, which is drawn by bisecting the right-angle made by the two axes at the origin. *ON* is sometimes known as the 45° line.[3] At every point along *ON*, *E* and *Y* have the

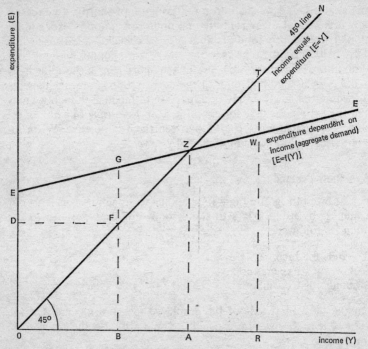

*Figure 7.4* The determination of equilibrium income

same value. At *F*, for instance, OB = OD, etc. That is the geometry. The economic significance of the line *ON* is straightforward. Since we know that equilibrium income must occur at a level at which total planned expenditure exactly matches income, it follows that equilibrium must lie at some point along *ON*.

However, we have already drawn a curve of planned expenditure *EE*, which describes the community's desired spending at different income levels. If plans are to be realised, the equilibrium income must also lie along *EE*. There is only one value of income that can satisfy

3. The equation of *ON* is *E* = *Y*.

the two conditions that it lie along both $ON$ and along $EE$. It is where the two lines cross at $Z$. Hence equilibrium income is $OA$.

Consider the implications of this conclusion. When $Y = OA$, the line $EE$ tells us that planned $E = AZ$. But $Z$ is on the 45° line; therefore $AZ = OA$. In other words, the community's planned expenditure, the sole constituent of which is here consumption, precisely matches its income. Hence income generated by expenditure is exactly equal to the income that it came from. $OA$ must be the equilibrium level of income.

The mechanism by which equilibrium is reached may be further clarified by supposing that income happens not to be at the equilibrium level. If income is above equilibrium, say at $OR$, we know from the aggregate demand curve $EE$ that the community will plan to spend only $RW$ of its income. This expenditure is less than income (by $WT$). Hence if only $WR$ is spent, the income generated will also be $WR$—i.e. less than $OR$, the original income. Income will therefore tend to fall. On the other hand, suppose that we start with a level of income which is below equilibrium, say $OB$. Planned expenditure corresponding to income $OB$ is $BG$, which is greater than $OB$ (by $FG$). Therefore, if $BG$ is spent, income will tend to rise. The only level of income which will be self-sustaining, which will generate expenditure equal to itself and at which spending plans match income, is $OA$.

## Savings and investment

It is now time to relax the highly unrealistic assumption that consumption is the only component of aggregate demand. We already know something about the other important categories of expenditure—investment, government, and exports. We shall for the moment, however, continue to deal with a closed economy without a government sector. Our concern is with a model economy in which expenditure must be either on consumption or on investment, for which we shall now use the symbol $I$.

Once more, let us start with a schematic representation of the conditions for equilibrium. As before, equilibrium will still obtain if the community's total expenditure plans precisely match its income. The only difference is that we have now to contend with an investment as well as a consumption component of total expenditure. In terms of Figure 7.5. equilibrium income is where the two blocks are equal in size.

Figure 7.5 is, however, severely deficient as a representation of

income

expenditure

*Figure 7.5* Income and expenditure

expenditure flows, because it assumes that investment and consumption decisions are made by the same persons. We shall find it more helpful, now that we have two expenditure categories, to revive the two decision-making categories we used before, households and businesses. We further assume:

i. that all income accrues to households, who are responsible for all consumption decisions;

ii. that planned investment is always the same—that investment determinants, not shown in our model, are unchanging;

iii. that all investment decisions are made by businesses. As businesses retain no income of their own, they can only pay for their investment expenditure by borrowing. Therefore, there must be:

iv. some institutions, such as banks, to make loans to businesses for investment expenditure.

Finally, we define all income *not* spent on consumption as **saving**, which we denote with the letter $S$—i.e. by definition: [4]

$$S = Y - C$$

Figure 7.6 presents a schematic representation of expenditure flows in our economy in equilibrium which, though greatly simplified, exactly fits our assumptions. All income accrues to households, who plan either to spend it on consumption or to save it. (By definition they cannot do anything else.) Investment expenditure is made by businesses, who finance their operations by borrowing. If you understood Figures 7.1, 7.2, and 7.3, you can tell at a glance that because

4. Readers of some other texts will note that $S = Y - C$ is a definition, and the proper way of expressing a definition (or 'identity') symbolically is by using a three bar 'equals' sign $\equiv$. Hence $S \equiv Y - C$ is the correct way of writing this. For further discussion of this matter see A. G. Ford, *Income, Spending and the Price Level*, Chapter 2, in this series.

the rectangle representing expenditure plans is equal in size to the income rectangle, you can rightly conclude that income is at equilibrium. The only new feature is that expenditure is divided into two components, consumption and business investment, in Figure 7.6.

But there is another very important conclusion to be drawn. Not only does total planned expenditure match original (*ex post*) income, but planned saving is equal to planned investment. This makes good enough sense. If households want to withold or abstain from consumption exactly that amount of total income which businesses want to use for investment, then it is natural that expenditure plans *must* match original income.

The necessary condition for income to be in equilibrium is that

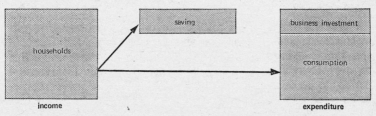

income                                                  expenditure

*Figure 7.6* Income and expenditure flows, savings equal to investment

the amount the community does *not* want to spend on consumption must be equal to the amount it wishes to spend on investment. But not consuming is, by definition, equal to saving. Therefore, the equilibrium condition can be alternatively stated as *planned (ex ante) savings must equal planned (ex ante) investment.*

There is nothing very new about this statement. It does no more than put in different language the condition we already know, namely that planned expenditure $(C + I)$ must be equal to original income. We can even reinterpret income in Figure 7.1 and income $OA$ in Figure 7.4, where no investment was allowed in the model, as being equilibrium situations because savings plans were implicitly zero.

The manner of expressing equilibrium is, however, novel, and may take a while to grasp. It is the key to the understanding of macroeconomics. Let us try to get used to the idea by examining it again when income is *not* at an equilibrium level.

Figure 7.7 illustrates the situation when original income is above equilibrium. We can now put this in either of two ways by saying either that planned expenditure is less than orignal income, or that planned savings are greater than planned investment. The business community want to spend on investment less than households want to give up consuming (i.e. to save). Hence there is a surplus left over from income that no one wants to spend. Total expenditure does not amount to as much as original income. Income does not, as it were, reproduce itself, but tends to fall.

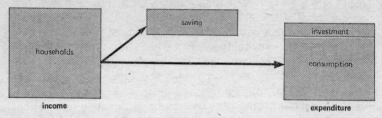

*Figure 7.7* Income and expenditure flows, savings greater than investment

Figure 7.8 illustrates the reverse situation, where planned investment exceeds planned saving. Now the business community wants to spend more on investment than households want not to consume (i.e. to save). There is not enough original income (*ex post* from the last period) to do this. If consumption is going to be as high as households want, then business can invest in real terms only the amount that they plan to invest by borrowing from the bank more than households wanted to save to finance their investment expenditure. Incomes tend to rise.

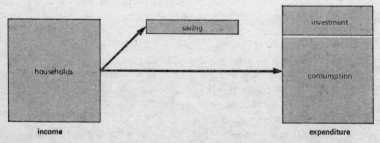

*Figure 7.8* Income and expenditure flows, investment greater than saving

Let us consider all three of these cases in our familiar graphical argument. Figure 7.9 is in two parts (i) and (ii). We look first only at part (i) which has axes, scale, and a 45° line drawn exactly as Figure 7.4. Furthermore, the line $CC$ approximates the aggregate expenditure in line $EE$ in Figure 7.4 where, since we previously defined expenditure as being the same as consumption, investment was zero. The only new feature is that investment is now positive. We are assuming,

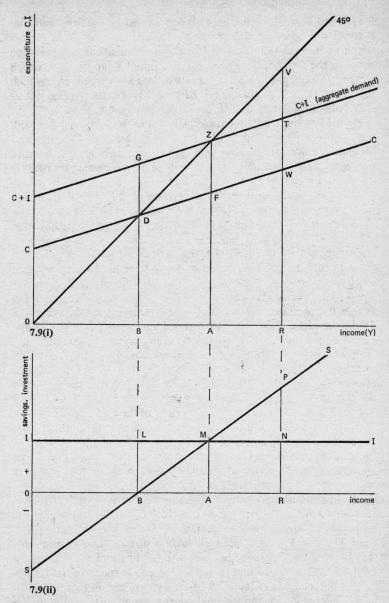

*Figure 7.9* The determination of equilibrium income, savings equals investment

for the moment, that investment is for a constant amount, and that it is not related at all to income, but is dependent on other factors which we leave out of account. Planned investment can be seen to be equal to the difference between the two lines $CC$ and $C + I$, which represents aggregate demand. The two lines are, moreover, parallel, so investment is always $GD (= ZF = TW)$—i.e. the vertical difference between $CC$ and $C + I$, regardless of income.

Planned savings are not directly measurable from the diagram, but if we remember that the 45° line shows equality of income and expenditure, we can measure savings plans by taking the difference between planned consumption and income. For instance, if income is $OR (= RV)$, planned consumption expenditure is $WR$. Therefore, planned savings must be $VW$. If income is $OA (= AZ)$, planned saving is $ZF$. If income is $OB (= BD)$, planned saving is zero; while if income is less than $OB$, planned saving is negative—people plan to spend more than their income.

Equilibrium income is at $OA$, where the aggregate demand curve $(C + I)$ cuts the 45° line, because at this level the community as a whole plans to spend on all forms of goods and services an amount equal to its income. We can see this is saying exactly the same thing as that the equilibrium level of income is where planned saving (the 45° line minus $ZF$) is equal to planned investment (the $C + I$ line minus $ZF$). If income is above equilibrium, say at $OR$, planned saving ($WV$) is greater than planned investment ($WT$). Income tends, therefore, to fall. If income is below equilibrium, say at $OB$, planned investment (still the same $DG$) is greater than planned saving, which is zero. Income tends therefore to rise.

Finally, let us look at the lower portion of the Figure, 7·9 (ii). This portrays precisely the same relationships in a slightly different way. We measure income on the horizontal axis, as before; but, instead of showing consumption and investment on the vertical axis, we show savings and investment directly. The scales of the graph in Figure 7.9 (ii) are exactly the same as in the upper portion (i).

The line for planned investment expenditure is now $II$, which is drawn parallel to the income axis, because planned investment expenditure is always the same ($BL = AM = RN = GD = ZF = TW$). The line $SS$ shows planned savings directly, and corresponds therefore to the difference between the $CC$ line and the 45° line in Figure 7.9 (i). For instance, when all income is spent on consumption, at $OB$ income in Figure 7.9 (i), savings are zero in Figure 7.9 (ii). When income is $OR$ and planned consumption is $RW$ in Figure 7.9 (i), planned saving is $WV$, which is equal to $PR$ in Figure 7.9 (ii).

Equilibrium income in Figure 7.9 (ii) is still $OA$, where savings and investment plans coincide, since $SS$ here intersects $II$. At incomes greater than $OA$, planned savings exceed planned investment, and income tends to fall. At incomes below $OA$, planned investment exceeds planned savings and income tends to rise.

### The role of stocks

The meaning of the equilibrium level of income should now be clear. So should the general tendency for upward and downward changes in income to occur when planned investment is greater or less than planned saving. There is only one other basic matter to understand about the theory of income determination. This involves the mechanism by which income moves towards equilibrium. Up till now, we have deliberately oversimplified the argument by ignoring an important component of actual investment. By definition, investment must embrace all production other than that which is consumed. Realised investment includes, therefore, changes in **stocks** of consumer goods in the hands of businesses.

Return now to the main argument and suppose, for example, that income is below the equilibrium level. Planned expenditure on consumption plus planned investment is greater than original income—i.e. planned investment is greater than planned saving. If consumers succeed in achieving their consumption plans, *and* if investors make all their planned capital expenditures, it follows that the stock of goods held by businesses must have fallen. This *unplanned* reduction in stocks is, as previously stated, a part of realised investment. Moreover, the difference between the totals of realised investment and of planned investment must measure this change in stocks. If you like to think of it another way, the unplanned reduction in stocks explains how realised investment could be less than planned investment.

This approach suggests a new way of thinking about income determination.[5] When income is below equilibrium, stocks fall off; we can appreciate, therefore, that businesses will tend to increase production in order to restore stocks to their previous level (provided, of course, there are no other changes in investment plans, which we

5. It also explains the following. (Let $S_p$, $S_r$, $I_p$, $I_r$ stand for planned and realised $S$ and $I$). We have assumed $I_p < S_p$, but we know that $I_r = S_r$. However, something must give way, $I_p$ or $S_p$. In the text we assume consumption plans are achieved, then $S_r = S_p$ and $I_r$ cannot possibly be equal to $I_p$. Rather $I_r < I_p$. The difference between them is the unplanned reduction in stocks.

assumed would not occur). The increase in production to replace unforeseen reductions in stocks requires extra factors of production. Businesses, therefore, hire more labour and other factors, paying them additional incomes. Hence, total income tends to rise, following an unplanned reduction in stocks, until it reaches equilibrium.

The argument applies in reverse when income happens to be above equilibrium—i.e. where planned saving exceeds investment. If, now, consumers spend only what they planned, while the business community spends on capital goods only what they planned, expenditure does not absorb all of original income, and businesses find an unplanned build-up of their stocks. On this occasion, the reaction of businesses must be to lay off workers and close down parts of factories, so as to allow stocks to fall to the lower, desired level. This action, however, sets in motion a downward movement in income.

### The so-called paradox of thrift

We must not forget that our ultra-simple model economy is very unrealistic. To mirror the real world it would need much elaboration and the addition of other determinants of every component of total expenditure. The models developed by Keynes to explain the causes of economic depression were, however, not much more involved than ours. The important new perspective from which Keynesian models view the working of the economy was obtained by focusing attention on aggregate demand, and on the way in which total expenditure determines income. Equilibrium is defined in terms of the level towards which income tends. It is not necessarily full employment income at all. We can appreciate some of the meaning of this statement by examining what is known as the paradox of thrift.

The paradox concerns the effect on total savings of an attempt by the community to save more than previously. We make all the assumptions with which we are now familiar, and use Figure 7.10, which is virtually identical to Figure 7.9 (ii). We shall introduce only one convenient term that has not been used before. It is this. The line SS has been described so far as the line of planned savings. It is also often referred to as a graphical expression of the **propensity to save** (or the '**savings function**'). As we know, SS represents the quantity of saving desired by the community at each income. If income is assumed to be at any given level (say $OA$) we call the relationship between planned saving ($AG$) and income ($OA$) the propensity to save. To be even more precise, we refer to the ratio $\dfrac{AG}{OA}$ as the **average pro-**

pensity to save. There is a similar definition for the **average propensity to consume** (or the '**consumption function**'). In Figure 7.9 (i), at income $OA$, the average propensity to consume is $\dfrac{AF}{OA}$.

In Figure 7.10 planned saving is equal to planned investment at income $OA$. Assume now we start at equilibrium, and that there is an

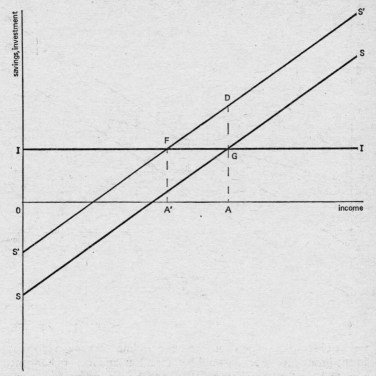

*Figure 7.10* The paradox of thrift, investment constant

increase in planned saving. People want to save more at every level of income than they did before. $SS$ shifts to $S'S'$. Planned saving now exceeds planned investment (i.e. $AD > AG$), so income tends to fall, until it reaches $OA'$, where savings and investment plans match each other ($A'F = A'F$). Hence the paradox: realised savings ($A'F$) are exactly the same as before ($AG$).

The clue to understanding why the desire by the community to save more did not increase total savings is to appreciate that it led to a *decrease in income*. At the lower income level people want to save less. Income stops falling only when it reaches the level at which planned savings equal planned investment. Note, incidentally, that the argument goes some way to explaining why a fall in aggregate demand (e.g. when the propensity to save increases) leads to declining incomes.

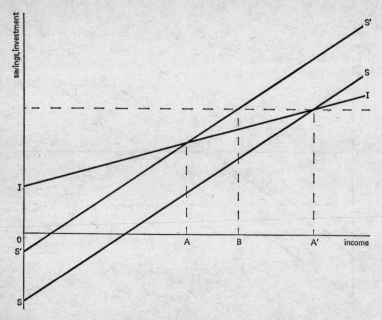

*Figure 7.11* The paradox of thrift, $I = f(y)$

The observed tendency for income to decline following an increase in the propensity to save would be more dramatic if there happened also to be a tendency for investment to be dependent on income. Suppose, for instance, that falling incomes lead to declining investment, i.e. that investment is a function of income. The line of planned investment would not then be parallel to the horizontal axis. It would have an upward slope, like that of *II* in Figure 7.11, which portrays a positive association between income and investment. That diagram shows, too, that an increase in the propensity to save, such as from *SS* to *S'S'*, would lead to a bigger fall in income than would take place if investment did not decline when income fell.

## The multiplier

When a slump occurs, as it did in the 1930s, incomes tend to fall sharply. We can see one reason why from the second version of the paradox of thrift. Aggregate demand falls off, because of an increase in the propensity to save (or a fall in planned investment). The level of income then declines, giving rise, in turn, to a reduction in investment. Moreover, it can be shown that a fall in investment causes a decline in income even greater than the fall in investment itself. The relationship between a change in investment, written as $\Delta I$, and a consequent change in income, written as $\Delta Y$, between two equilibrium positions, is termed the **multiplier**.

The simplest way to explain the working of the multiplier is to introduce a last piece of terminology relating to the propensity to consume. Previously, we defined the average propensity to consume (A.P.C.) at any level of income as $\frac{C}{Y}$, and the average propensity to save (A.P.S.) as $\frac{S}{Y}$. We now define the **marginal propensities to consume and to save** as the *changes* in consumption and saving relative to the *change* in income, or $\frac{\Delta C}{\Delta Y}$ and $\frac{\Delta S}{\Delta Y}$.

An example may help to make these definitions clear. Suppose that when income rises from 1,000 to 2,000, consumption rises from 900 to 1,500. We can calculate the average and marginal propensities to consume by means of Table 7.1:

Table 7.1   **Calculation of the propensity to consume and to save**

| | *Income* | |
|---|---|---|
| | 1,000 | 2,000 |
| Average $(APC)\frac{(C)}{(Y)}$ | $\frac{900}{1,000} = 0\cdot9$ | $\frac{1,500}{2,000} = 0\cdot75$ |
| Average $(APS)\frac{(S)}{(Y)}$ | $\frac{100}{1,000} = 0\cdot1$ | $\frac{500}{1,000} = 0\cdot25$ |
| Marginal $MPC\frac{(\Delta C)}{(\Delta Y)}$ | | $\frac{1,500 - 900}{2,000 - 1,000} = 0\cdot6$ |
| Marginal $MPS\frac{(\Delta S)}{(\Delta Y)}$ | | $\frac{500 - 100}{2,000 - 1,000} = 0\cdot4$ |

(Note that the $MPS + MPC = 1 = APS + APC$, because income can only be saved or consumed.)

Return now to our definition of the multiplier, $\dfrac{\Delta Y}{\Delta I}$. Suppose investment rises by 100. Incomes of the factors of production rise at once by 100. What happens to the extra 100 of income now created? The answer is that some of it is spent, and creates additional income, and some is saved. How much of each? The M.P.S. and the M.P.C. tell us the answer.

Suppose, as in our example in Table 7.1, the M.P.S. $= 0.4$ and M.P.C. $= 0.6$. Then an income rise of 100 leads to 40 more saving and to 60 more consumption. An increase in income of 100 will cause income to rise, therefore, by 160 (60 more than the original 100). But the process does not stop there. The extra 60 of income will again either be spent or saved, according to the M.P.C. and the M.P.S. So the full rise in income, given that we are not worried about how long it takes, is a series:

$$100 + 6/10\,(100) + 6/10 \times 6/10\,(100) + \ldots, \text{etc.}$$
$$\text{or } 100 + 6/10\,(100) + 6/10^2\,(100) + \ldots 6/10^n\,(100)$$
$$\text{or } 100 + 60 + 36 + 21.6 + \ldots, \text{etc.}$$

The series is an infinite one which gradually approaches the limit, 250. If an increase in investment of 100 causes an increase of income of 250, the multiplier is said to be $2\frac{1}{2}$ $\left( \dfrac{\Delta Y}{\Delta I} = \dfrac{250}{100} = 2.5 \right)$.

It may not have escaped the reader's attention that the multiplier is the marginal propensity to save upside down (its reciprocal).[6] We may be satisfied with the realisation that there is a perfect, though inverse, relationship between the multiplier and the M.P.S. This is natural enough. Only expenditure creates income. Savings are a kind of leakage. The greater the amount of saving from any given change in income, the less extra income is created. If, for instance, the M.P.C. was $\frac{1}{2}$, and the M.P.S. also therefore $\frac{1}{2}$, the stream of new

6. Two quick proofs of this reciprocal relationship are:

i. The infinite series $1 + C\,(1) + C^2\,(1) + C^3\,(1) + \ldots$ has the solution $\dfrac{1}{1 - C}$ (if $1 > C > 0$). $\dfrac{1}{1 - C}$ is, of course, $\dfrac{1}{\text{the M.P.S}}$.

ii. The multiplier is $\dfrac{\Delta Y}{\Delta I}$. We know, however, that $\Delta Y = \Delta I + \Delta C$, and therefore that $\Delta I = \Delta Y - \Delta C$. The multiplier may then be written $\dfrac{\Delta Y}{\Delta Y - \Delta C}$ which is $\dfrac{1}{1 - \dfrac{\Delta C}{\Delta Y}} = \dfrac{1}{\dfrac{\Delta S}{\Delta Y}}$.

A third, geometric, proof is given in the next footnote.

incomes created would be $100 + 50 + 25 + 12\frac{1}{2}$, etc., approaching 200. The multiplier would be only 2.

Figure 7.12 gives a graphical representation of the multiplier. An increase in investment from $II$ to $I'I'$ raises incomes from $OA$ to $OA'$, The

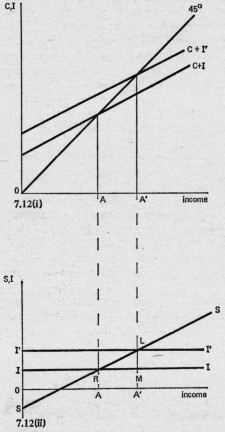

7.12(i)

7.12(ii)

*Figure 7.12* The multiplier

multiplier therefore is $\dfrac{\Delta Y}{\Delta I} = \dfrac{AA'}{LM} = \dfrac{RM}{LM}$. Moreover, the M.P.S., $\dfrac{\Delta S}{\Delta Y}$,

appears on the graph as the slope, or gradient, of the line $SS$. The steeper the line the more savings increase as income rises, i.e. the greater the M.P.S. and the less the M.P.C. Hence, if you drew a steeper line going through point $R$, and assumed that investment rose as in Figure 7.12, you would find that the ensuing increase in income was less than in the diagram. The multiplier would be smaller because the M.P.S. was greater.[7]

The multiplier process helps in understanding the way in which a slump can snowball downwards. If falling incomes lead to falling investment, the severity of the slump is likely to be greater than otherwise. All this is what might be called the economics of depression, when income is at a low equilibrium level with mass unemployment. But the multiplier can also work upwards in the reverse direction. Once a boom gets going with an increase in expenditure, there is an upward multiplier effect on income. This can lead to a further increase in investment, which will raise incomes again and feed on itself. In these ways the upswings and downswings of the trade cycle can get going.

More difficult to explain are turning points of the cycle—why a slump burns itself out and the economy moves out of stagnation into an upswing, or from a boom into a crisis.

Historically, each cycle has differed from others, and almost the only generalisation that can be made about turning points is that they are sharper and shorter in duration than boom and slump periods. Crises can start in many ways: with sudden, even irrational, drops in business confidence; with declining investment opportunities or cost increases as a boom continues; with overseas developments; with the activities of the government; and many more. Slumps can turn upwards for the opposite reasons and we cannot pretend to deal adequately with them here. Suffice it to say that economists find the forecasting of cyclical turning points among their more difficult tasks.

## Full employment and the price level

At the beginning of our analysis of the determination of national income we made the explicit assumption of a constant price level. We must now take a step towards reality in order to take a very brief glimpse at the causes of changes in the general level of prices. To do so, we start with Figure 7.13.

Figure 7.13 is not a direct statement of statistics about prices in any country for any particular period of time. But it is a schematic

7. This is a third proof that the multiplier is $\frac{1}{\text{M.P.S.}}$. In Figure 7.12 the multiplier is defined as $RM/LM$, and the M.P.S. as $LM/RM$.

representation of what is widely thought to be the relationship between the general price level and output. It assumes that the level of income corresponding to full employment is *OF*. Below this level there are unused resources (e.g. unemployed labour and idle capital) available for business to draw upon if aggregate demand rises.

In other words, supply is able to expand and keep pace with an increasing demand without affecting the general price level. As full employment is approached (at output *OF*), however, the situation

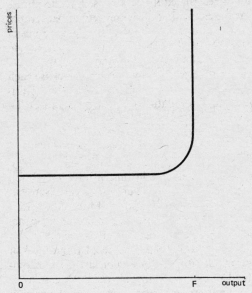

*Figure 7.13* Output and the general price level

changes and bottlenecks begin to appear. Some prices start to rise. If aggregate demand continues to increase, eventually no unused resources remain. So the full effect of the increased demand is seen only in rising prices, or **inflation**.

One cause of inflationary price increases is, therefore, an increase of aggregate demand at full employment. Turn back for a moment to Figure 7.12. Suppose full employment income is *OA*—i.e., at *OA*, real national income is at a maximum. An increase of aggregate demand from $C + I$ to $C + I'$, in Figure 7.12 (i), would then cause an **inflationary gap** to appear.[8] Income would tend to rise, to *OA'*, *in*

8. In fact the excess of aggregate demand over income at full employment is sometimes defined as the inflationary gap.

*money terms only*, because the general price level would increase because the economy was at a point similar to *OF* in Figure 7.13.

Notice incidentally that the inflationary gap may appear without any actual price increases. There is **inflationary pressure**, which may, perhaps, be temporarily concealed by price controls, and appeals to businesses and trade unions not to raise prices and wages. In such circumstances inflation would be said to be **suppressed**, to distinguish it from **open** inflation, when prices rise freely.

The reader may have noticed the caution expressed in the phrase 'one cause of inflation' at the beginning of the preceding paragraph. Economists have advanced a number of different explanations of inflationary processes. One school of thought sees rising costs of production as a prime cause of inflation. We cannot deal with this matter now. It is true that costs, prices, and wages tend to chase each other upwards when inflation gets going, but the problem of identifying the causal element during an inflationary process can rarely be solved satisfactorily.

## More realistic assumptions

We have now come as far as is possible in this introductory book with the analysis of macroeconomic behaviour. The great disadvantage of stopping here is that we cannot consider all the implications for our theories of a variety of complicated, but more realistic, assumptions. For example, we have so far assumed that the effect of a change in income on consumption is not affected by the level of income—i.e. that the marginal propensity to consume is constant—whereas it may well tend to decline as income rises. We can, however, list some of the more important factors, other than the level of income, on which the propensity to save (and therefore the propensity to consume) depends.[9] They include:

Psychological motives (e.g. the desire to build up a fortune); the availability of credit institutions (e.g. hire purchase); the size and age distribution of the population; technological advance (new production techniques and new products); advertising; the stock of wealth; the distribution of income, and its past as well as its present level.

We should also add something more about determinants of investment expenditure to make the theory more realistic. Investment has

9. We must also be careful to avoid the fallacy of composition, see below p. 205.

so far been assumed to be largely determined by outside forces, some of which were discussed in Chapter 5—the rate of interest and the state of business confidence. Moreover, investment may be influenced by income, the availability of credit, and technological advance. It should be emphasised, too, that investment demand is dependent on *expectations* of the future profitability of capital investment, which can be highly volatile, and affected by rumours, overseas events, and many other social and political factors.

The only general matter worth emphasising here about the diversity of the determinants of savings and investment is that the decisions about each of them are made not only for different reasons but by quite different persons and institutions. There is no reason to believe that market forces will always and automatically bring about an exact coincidence of the savings plans of households and businesses with the investment plans of businesses.[10] Moreover, since consumption tends to be a fairly steady function of income, while investment demand is (for reasons advanced above) more unstable, fluctuations in expenditure are frequently attributed to changes in investment, rather than to changes in consumption.

## Stabilisation

We now turn from an analysis of theory to a discussion of policy. Early in the chapter we emphasised that fluctuations in income and expenditure have historically followed a rhythmical pattern, known as the trade cycle. It is obvious how important it is to try to reduce the amplitude of upward and downward swings of the cycle by manipulating the level of aggregate demand. No periods of prolonged heavy unemployment, like that of the 1930s, have occurred since the Second World War, partly because governments have attempted to stabilise the level of income in the economy—or at least to stabilise its rate of growth.

10. We are also deliberately ignoring the possibility that some market forces may help to prevent fluctuations in income. Pre-Keynesian economic theory (dubbed 'classical' by Keynes) emphasised quite a different relationship. An excess of savings over investment in the classical system led to a fall in the rate of interest, which in turn induced more investment to take up the slack. No decline in aggregate demand followed, and income remained unchanged. Many combinations and extensions of Keynes' and classical assumptions have been developed, but cannot be discussed here. Moreover, there can be little doubt that the simple model of macroeconomic behaviour presented in the text, though by no means always applicable, can provide a disproportionately profound insight into many real world situations, past and present.

There are three main stabilisation techniques open to a government. One is **monetary policy**, which was discussed in Chapter 5. The second policy focuses attention on the size of a government's budget; increasing government spending (or reducing taxation) when income is considered to be too low; budgeting for a surplus of income over expenditure when the danger is of inflation rather than of slump. The third technique concentrates on the size of the private element in demand. The government may try to alter the structure of taxation, for example, by reducing corporation profits tax in order to stimulate private investment. Alternatively, institutions may be set up and given powers over prices and incomes, so as to influence aggregate private demand. The last of these techniques is usually referred to by the special name of **incomes policy**.

**Fiscal policy** is the term used to describe government stabilisation activity through budgetary means. It is immensely difficult to put successfully into practice. We shall return to the subject again in the next chapter. Meanwhile, it may be observed in advance that stabilisation is not a simple policy goal for a state to pursue, and that post-war British governments have been more successful in preventing the onset of deep depressions than in avoiding inflationary pressures. At the same time, the government has been aiming at the promotion of economic growth, a goal which can call for quite different, and perhaps contradictory, policies.

### The components of total aggregate demand

We began the discussion of national income determination with the assumption that the only element in aggregate demand was consumption expenditure, thus:

$$E = C \qquad . \quad . \quad . \quad . \quad . \quad . \quad . \quad . \quad . \quad . \quad . \quad . \quad . \quad . \quad 1$$

We then added investment expenditure to have a more realistic model where:

$$E = C + I \qquad . \quad . \quad . \quad . \quad . \quad . \quad . \quad . \quad . \quad . \quad . \quad . \quad 2$$

Then, in the last section, we admitted that government expenditure on goods and services ($G$) should be added to the total.[11] In other words:

$$E = C + I + G \qquad . \quad . \quad . \quad . \quad . \quad . \quad . \quad . \quad . \quad . \quad 3$$

11. The way in which the government finances its expenditure—by taxation or by borrowing, for example—can also influence the level of aggregate demand, through the effect on the propensity to consume and on private investment.

Finally, we must allow for international implications. Expenditure by foreigners on exports $(X)$ is quite as income-generating for British businesses as domestic expenditure on home sales. Purchases of imports $(M)$ by British consumers, on the other hand, do not create incomes in this country. So it would be sensible to write:

$$E = C + I + G + (X-M) \qquad \qquad \qquad 4$$

In words, this equation says that aggregate demand comprises consumption demand, investment demand, government expenditure on goods and services, and any export surplus. (The last item can, of course, be negative.)

We must draw one conclusion from this more comprehensive statement of the component of aggregate demand. It is no longer true that equilibrium income occurs at the level where planned savings is equal to planned investment. That formulation applied only to a closed economy without a government.

We can, however, restate the equilibrium condition in a convenient form. Let us group together the income flows which, like savings, are **leakages** from the economy. They are $S$ and $M$, and they may be described as leakages because they do not generate income. Next, we can group together **injections** of expenditure which do add to the flow of incomes. They are $I$, $G$, and $X$. The condition for income to be in equilibrium remains the same—that aggregate demand or planned expenditure is equal to original income (or to planned production). However, equilibrium no longer corresponds to the same equality of planned savings and investment; but of planned injections and planned withdrawals. Our reformulated equilibrium condition for an economy with both a government and an international sector is, therefore:

planned $S + M$ is equal to planned $I + G + X$.[12]

12. Formal statements of the multiplier, the paradox of thrift, etc., should also be rewritten for an open economy with a government sector. See A. G. Ford, *Income, Spending and the Price Level*, Chapter 4.

# Chapter 8

# Economic Policy

## Government revenue and expenditure

The British government, central and local, currently raises in revenue an annual sum amounting to approximately 40–50 per cent of the national income. The precise figure is not important. Indeed, the part played by the state in the economic life of the country cannot be

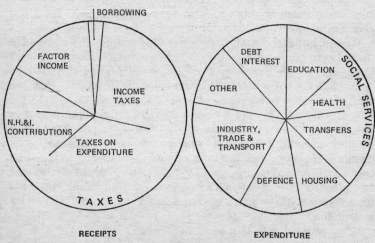

RECEIPTS                    EXPENDITURE

*Figure 8.1* Government finances, 1969. Expenditure and receipts on current and capital account of combined public authorities.
Source: *National Income and Expenditure,* (H.M.S.O. 1970)

measured simply by the size of its budget in money terms; but it is instructive to take a look at the *relative* importance of the chief ways in which the government raises funds and spends them (see Figure 8.1).

## Government revenue

The government gets its income in three principal ways—by levying taxes, by selling goods and services, and by borrowing.

i. *Taxes* account for more than three-quarters of the total receipts of the government. The main revenue raisers are taxes on the incomes of persons (income tax and surtax), and of companies (e.g. corporation tax), and taxes on expenditure (e.g. duties on alcohol, tobacco, petrol, and purchase tax). Taxes may also be raised on capital (e.g. death duties), the employment of labour (e.g. selective employment tax), and other items. Compulsory levies on individuals which are directly related to government expenditure on social services are also made. They are substantial sources of income, and are known as national insurance and national health contributions.

ii. *Factor income* provides a secondary source of revenue for the government. Any receipts, such as revenue from bus services or rent and interest from government property, or proceeds of the sale of goods and services provided by state-owned factors of production, would be included under this head. The revenues of the nationalised industries should also be classed as factor incomes, though they are kept financially separate from other government receipts.

iii. *Borrowing*. The government finances a part of its expenditure by short or long-term borrowing, through the issue (i.e. sales) of government securities to the public. Capital expenditure is sometimes financed this way in normal times, and borrowing has been the prime means of paying for war expenditures. The outstanding total of government securities is known as the National (or Public) Debt, and is about as large as the annual national income. The enormous size of the national debt may be superficially alarming, but it does not in fact constitute a major burden around a country's neck, as is sometimes suggested, because there is no obligation on the government to repay the total. Nobody expects the state to do more than pay the accruing interest to holders of government securities. As any particular block of loans matures and must be repaid, the government almost always meets this obligation by floating a new loan.

## Government expenditure

There are several alternative and useful ways of looking at the components of government expenditure. Figure 8.1 makes the division according to function or purpose, and brings out the relative size of expenditure on the social services and housing, a substantial part of which is by local authorities. The item described as industry and trade consists chiefly of investment by the nationalised industries, but includes also help given to private industry, agriculture, and commerce.

Alternative breakdowns would emphasise different features. For instance, about three-quarters of all expenditure consists of current as distinct from capital items. Nearly a third of the total is made by local authorities, although a substantial proportion of their funds originates as grants from the central government, and the distinction must therefore be treated with reserve.

Finally and significantly, attention must be drawn to the fact that less than half of total expenditure is on goods and services. The remainder comprises **transfers** of money to the private sector, substantially in the form of retirement pensions, social benefits, and interest on the national debt. To the extent that transfers are financed by taxes, they represent merely a redistribution of income by the government. They may be contrasted with so-called **exhaustive** expenditures on goods and services. Only these latter expenditures constitute demands by the public sector on the real resources available in the economy. In the light of this information, we may usefully review the opening sentence of this chapter. The share of the national product pre-empted, as it were, by the government, is much closer to a quarter than to a half of the national product. The total of government expenditure, however measured, has nevertheless been growing significantly for many years. The growth has more than kept pace with rising prices and increasing population. The phenomenon of an expanding government sector has not been confined to Britain, and in an important way it has mirrored contemporary opinion about the role of the state in economic affairs. The remainder of this chapter discusses the rationale of government intervention in the economy.

### The case for *laissez-faire*

The first question which might reasonably be asked about economic policy is why it is needed in the first place. The question is a very pertinent one, because the material in Chapters 3 and 4 suggested that a freely working price system might manage, unaided, to bring about a satisfactory distribution of resources. The argument in favour of free enterprise is sometimes known as the case for *laissez-faire* (which might be liberally translated from the French as 'leave alone').

The argument may be briefly restated. If we assume that consumers always adjust their expenditure on goods so as to maximise their satisfaction, given their tastes and the relative prices of the goods and services available to them, then we may infer that the price that is paid at the margin (i.e. by a consumer who only just finds it worth while buying one more unit of a product) is a measure of the satisfaction he derives from a good. In other words, price measures marginal utility.

We now add the further assumption that producers always maximise their profits, given the prices of the factors of production and consumer demands. Producers find their optimum outputs where the marginal cost of producing a good is equal to the marginal revenue received from selling it. Provided each producer can sell as much as he wants at the market price, marginal revenue must be equal to price. Therefore it is alleged the market brings about equality between price and marginal cost. In other words, the cost of producing the 'last' unit of each good is exactly the same as the satisfaction that it brings. If output were smaller, marginal cost would be less than marginal utility, so that an increase in production would be valued by consumers at a figure in excess of the extra cost that would be involved in producing it. Conversely, if outputs were larger than at the point where marginal cost equals marginal utility, a reduction in output would bring a larger fall in costs than in benefits.

Moreover, we must remember that costs in economics are real opportunity costs, measuring the sacrifices of goods not produced. Hence, no reallocation of resources between products can bring about a better pattern of production. Prices, acting as signals, direct resources to the uses which maximise the satisfaction of consumers. In such circumstances, it might be argued, interference with the freedom of the market mechanism to work towards the best allocation of resources is undesirable.

## The relevance of *laissez-faire*

The conclusion just derived, however, is not one about the real world, but comes from a model[1] of an economy based upon certain implicit and explicit assumptions about behaviour. If the assumptions of the model do not hold in reality, the relevance of the conclusion itself is thrown in doubt. Let us look, therefore, at each assumption in turn. If any one of them is unrealistic, we must have doubts about the applicability of the entire argument.

1. Models are discussed in some detail in Chapter 9.

i. 'Consumers maximise their satisfaction.' This is, perhaps, the most acceptable assumption. Consumers, one imagines, certainly want to maximise their satisfaction. They may not always succeed, however, and this is a material point to which we shall return later.

ii. 'Producers maximise profits.' Many producers probably do try to make as much profit as they can, at any rate in the long run. But some producers, especially large ones, may not need to aim for maximum profits at all. If they are significant in number, we may have serious doubts about the desirability of the allocation of resources brought about by a free market.

iii. 'Producers expand output until marginal cost is equal to price.' We know from Chapter 4 that a profit-maximising firm in conditions of perfect competition will produce the output at which marginal cost is equal to price. A monopolist, however, will maximise profits at a different (lower) level of output, at which marginal cost is equal to marginal revenue, which is less than price.

We can provisionally conclude, therefore, that the existence of imperfectly competitive markets may prevent a freely working price mechanism from leading to the best allocation of resources for consumers. But suppose every market consisted of large numbers of small firms, producing an identical product under conditions of perfect knowledge and of free entry into the industry. In other words, suppose that the assumptions of perfect competition applied to the real world. Let us ask whether that would be sufficient to realise optimum resource allocation. The answer is obviously still no, or we should not have asked it. The reasoning behind the answer, however, is very important. There is, in fact, a fourth implicit assumption underlying the argument in favour of non-intervention in the market place which must now be brought into the open:

iv. The satisfactions that individuals receive from purchases of goods and services as measured by the sums of money spent on them can be simply added together to obtain the total satisfaction of the community as a whole.

At first glance, this may seem acceptable enough, provided we are prepared to accept assumption (i). As we have argued more than once, if each consumer maximises his satisfaction in disposing of his income, he will buy goods in such quantities that the price he has to pay for an additional unit of each good is equal to the satisfaction he obtains from it. What then is the catch? Can we not add up the satisfactions of all individuals to get an estimate of total satisfaction? The answer is that we can, sometimes, but not always, because there are certain kinds of product that have what are called **external** effects. This means simply that their consumption or production by one individual affects the satisfaction of other individuals. We shall return to this point shortly. First, however, a cautionary word.

### Value judgments

When we discuss economic policy, we find it virtually impossible to avoid statements about the desirability or undesirability of particular policy objectives, such as full employment and a more or less equal distribution of income. Policy decisions can be reached only if someone is prepared to pronounce what we call **value judgments** on these largely controversial matters. For instance, if we consider a policy measure, such as the imposition of a new tax, we may be able to make a value-free prediction of its effect on the size of the national income. Suppose we are reasonably confident that the national income would rise, but that the benefit from this would fall on only a proportion of the population, while some people would actually lose from the effects of the tax. Someone, however, must decide whether or not the tax is to be imposed, and whoever does so will be forced to weigh, in principle, the benefits accruing to some individuals against the harm inflicted on others. There is no simple, perfect, way of doing so. Hence, he must make a value judgment.[1]

As economists, strictly speaking, we should try to leave the making of value judgments to others. This means that we may rarely find ourselves able to come to clear conclusions about the desirability of any particular policy. For example, even though it is easy to argue that the price mechanism is not a *perfect* resource allocator, we shall never be able to prove that there is any alternative way of allocating resources which is necessarily *better on all counts* than a system of *laissez faire*. Even if we make a pretty strong economic case, occasionally, for government interference, someone may object that it is undesirable, on political grounds, to give the government any more power. Each policy alternative must be considered on its merits.

### Market failure

After this warning, we may return to the task of examining the most important reasons why the price mechanism fails to act in an ideal manner to allocate resources between competing uses. Analysis of **market failure** may be destructive, but it is important because it can lead to policy proposals. If a doctor knows something about the causes of an illness as well as being able to recognise its symptoms.

1. Identifying value judgments is not always easy. See below pp. 179–82.

he will be more likely to make a cure than simply to relieve its adverse effects.

There are several acceptable ways of grouping together the causes of market failure. All inevitably involve some overlapping, and here we use a fivefold classification:

i. Market imperfections.
ii. Private and social values.
iii. Paternalism.
iv. The distribution of income and wealth.
v. Time and macroeconomic policy.

## Market imperfections

The price mechanism fails to bring about an ideal distribution of resources if, in any use, the marginal cost of a product is not equal

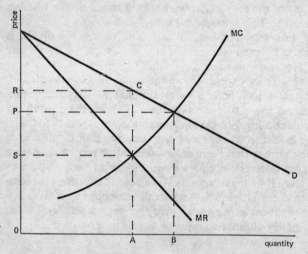

*Figure 8.2* Output of a profit maximising monopolist (*OA*) is less than competitive output (*OB*)

to its marginal utility. But this is exactly what we expect to occur in conditions of *im*perfect competition. It will be recalled from Chapter 4 that a monopolist maximises profit if he expands output only to the point at which marginal cost is equal to marginal revenue. In Figure 8.2, for example, at the monopoly output, *OA*, marginal cost is *OS*, while marginal utility is *OR*. Output is less than the optimal level, *OB*, at which marginal cost and marginal utility are both equal to price, *OP*. This is our first clear case of a freely working price system failing to distribute resources adequately.

We must not, however, leave the analysis here. The appearance of a monopolist element in an industry is not a purely random event. There are several causes of the creation of monopoly power, and a well thought out policy towards imperfection of competition must take account of the specific causes in each case.

A firm enjoys a degree of monopoly if it finds that it is able to set the price of its product at a different level from that of its rivals

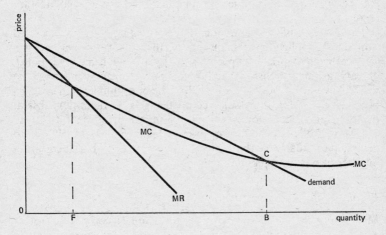

*Figure 8.3.* A 'natural' monopoly exists if marginal costs continue to decline before market demand is satisfied

without its sales falling to zero. Monopoly then depends on (*a*) the firm's size relative to the market for the industry, and (*b*) the extent to which its product is regarded by consumers as different from that of other producers. The latter cause is itself a function of the nature of the product (i.e. whether it is a book or a loaf of bread); the amount of advertising engaged in by the seller; and the extent to which consumers are aware of the true nature of the product (i.e. how well informed they are about it). The relative size of a firm which possesses monopoly power is not independent of the forces just discussed. Such power is related also to the institutional arrangements in a country and the extent to which independent firms are able, by amalgamating or collaborating through trade associations, to restrict the operation of competitive forces.

One further cause of large size deserves special mention. This is the case of the so called **natural** monopoly, which tends to appear in an industry if the nature of costs is such that they continue to fall over the range of relevant output. Figure 8.3 illustrates the case. It differs from Figure 8.2 only in that the marginal cost curve is declining when it intersects the demand curve, i.e. when the entire market demand is satisfied. Falling marginal costs are generally attributed to the need for the installation of a particularly expensive item of capital equipment before any output is forthcoming. An example might be the capital plant needed to manufacture nylon.

The presence of a natural monopoly poses a particularly awkward problem for policy-makers. Inevitably, the lowest cost way of producing the appropriate output must be by a single firm. Yet a policy of leaving a monopolist, even a low cost one, alone may mean that he will indulge in restricting output below the optimum level in order to boost profits. Moreover, since competition is by definition absent, the monopolist may not even try to be internally efficient and keep costs low. Policy in the face of monopolistic elements is difficult to devise, particularly in the natural monopoly case, but there are a number of ways of tackling the problem.

*Encouragement of competition*

Most countries try, to some extent, to stimulate competitive forces artificially. In Britain, a series of Acts of Parliament, starting in 1948 with the setting up of a Monopolies Commission and later a Restrictive Practices Court, have created machinery to deal with individual cases. Certain restrictive practices have been declared illegal —e.g. agreements by groups of manufacturers to fix jointly the prices at which their products are sold or *resold* (*Resale Price Maintenance*), and witholding supplies from traders who act against the wishes of the seller.

Many so-called restrictive practices, however, have both merits and demerits. The Restrictive Practices Court has the job of weighing the arguments of businesses which operate any of a wide range of monopolistic practices, and of judging whether or not they operate, on balance, against the public interest. A similar role has been played by the Monopolies Commission since 1948 in cases when a single large monopolist is present. One advantage claimed for this approach to monopoly regulation is that it enables a hard line to be taken in cases where costs are not obviously favourable to a dominant single firm (the Figure 8.2 type), and a softer line in case of natural monopolies (the Figure 8.3 type), provided the latent power is not abused. Unfortunately, the knowledge of the cost structures of firms necessary to the formation of the appropriate policy is not easy to obtain without a public investigation.

The effectiveness of British legislation against restrictive practices is difficult to assess. As each case is decided on an individual basis, it is necessary to look at the way in which the Restrictive Practices Court has interpreted the law. Experience here has been mixed. Some cases, especially in the early days, were decided in a competitive spirit (e.g. the case of the cotton yarn spinners), while decisions in others followed a more lenient line, with manufacturers being allowed to continue practices which have been regarded by some economists as being fairly clearly against the public interest (e.g. the cement case).

Mention should also be made of other ways in which competition is encouraged by government action. Most of these stem from a basic characteristic of imperfect competition—that its persistence is due to the existence of frictions or immobilities in the market which hinder changes in supply or demand. The frictions, in turn, are often the result of inadequate machinery for the exchange of information. Consumers are particularly badly informed about the quality of many competing products, though the growth of consumer organisations (whether or not it is encouraged by the government) and control of advertising may bring about some improvement.

We must also not overlook the fact that monopoly can be present in the labour market as well as in the market for goods. Legislation reducing the strength of trade unions is, however, politically quite a different matter from that aimed at promoting competition among businesses.

*Public regulation*

A second way of trying to influence the allocation of resources is by direct control of an industry by the state. Public regulation does not necessarily imply any change in ownership of a firm, but it does involve trying to influence its price or output policy.

In principle, provided cost and demand curves are known, it is possible to devise alternative policies which will even entice a (larger) competitive output from a monopolist. Referring again to Figure 8.2 (page 150), we could imagine a subsidy per unit produced being offered to a monopolist in such a way as to lower the marginal cost curve so as to ensure that it cuts the marginal revenue curve directly above *B*. At the same time, the government might impose a lump sum tax, equal to the subsidy but payable regardless of output. This could prevent the monopolist from benefiting at the taxpayers' expense. Alternatively, subsidies could be given to consumers. The amount would then need to be calculated in such a way as to shift the demand and marginal revenue curves upwards so that the latter cut the original marginal cost curve at output *OB*. A third method would simply fix price by law, at *OP*. This would effectively transform both demand and marginal revenue curves into a single horizontal line, as in perfect competition. Optimum output for the monopolist could then also be *OB*.

Arrangements of this nature are difficult to organise. Knowledge of both cost and demand curves are essential to their success, and their administration in a changing world can be very troublesome. Moreover, such schemes are rarely attractive politically.

## *Nationalisation*

The third and final major policy alternative for the control of monopoly is for the state itself to take over and run the business. Nationalisation is, of course, an exceedingly controversial political matter. Aside from politics, however, state ownership would generally be regarded as a more suitable solution in the natural monopoly case than in most others. If costs are such that a monopoly is the most efficient form of business in an industry, so the argument runs, then monopoly we must have; but let it be publicly rather than privately owned.

Once nationalised, however, an industry's problems are by no means over. Apart from questions of organisation and incentives, the same basic economic decisions have still to be made—what output to produce and what price to charge for it. A glance at Figure 8.3 (page 151) will suggest some of the problems here.

In Figure 8.3, optimum output is *OB*, at which marginal cost equals marginal utility. But in order to sell *OB* units, market price must be *CB*, and at this price the firm will not cover its full costs. This important feature of the situation is due to the fact that marginal cost is falling. Since price, as argued above, must be equal to marginal cost for optimum output, the business will certainly cover the cost of the marginal unit. But all the other units must make losses, because the same price is charged for them while their marginal cost is higher.[2]

There is no universally agreed way of dealing with this problem, which we cannot discuss in detail here. We may note, however, the inference that nationalised industries with falling costs may make losses in spite of operating efficiently and producing an appropriate output. The reason why any particular nationalised industry may be making losses is, of course, another question. Inefficient management may be the cause, and this is why a fair degree of public inspection and accountability is regarded as essential for nationalised industries.

This completes the discussion of market imperfections as a reason why the price mechanism works less than perfectly in allocating resources among competing uses. We now turn to the second reason, private and social values.

## Private and social values

Let us once again remind ourselves that price acts in a market as a signal of both the marginal benefit to consumers and the marginal cost of production of a good. Under the 'right' circumstances, as we have seen, the marginal cost to society of resources employed in producing a good is equated to price, which itself is a measure of the marginal utility, or benefit, that it gives.

Implicit in the argument is the idea that the price paid by a consumer for a good is a measure of the satisfaction which he gets from it. Provided the person buying a product is the only one benefiting from the purchase, and that the actual producer of the good is the only one who has to bear the costs of producing it, the price mechanism cannot be faulted on this count. For certain goods and services, the individuals buying and selling them are the only ones involved in costs and benefits. For other goods, however, price does not indicate benefit or cost *to society*, although it might perfectly well measure utility and cost to the private individual.

Let us take an example of two goods. Compare a service such as smallpox vaccination with one like a visit to a greyhound race meeting. When someone pays to attend a race meeting, the only consumer benefit we can reasonably expect to accrue is that to the person who goes there. This we term **private benefit**, although in fact it happens

2. In terms of the diagram, total revenue from *OB* sales at price *CB* is the area *OB* times *CB*. Total costs, however, consist of the sum of the marginal costs of every unit of output or, the area below the marginal cost curve.

also to be the **social benefit** to society as a whole, since no one else gets any satisfaction from his expenditure.

In the case of a smallpox vaccination, on the other hand, the benefit deriving from expenditure extends beyond that rendered to the person buying the service, in so far as it reduces the risk to other people of contracting the disease. In this case we say that there are what are called **external**, **spillover**, or **neighbourhood** effects, and that social benefits are greater than private benefits. Consequently, if the output of race meetings is expanded to the point where the marginal utility to the individual paying for the service is equal to the marginal cost of providing it, the price mechanism will result in exactly the 'right' numbers of race meetings. But if the same policy is applied to smallpox vaccinations, output will be expended only up to the point where marginal utility *to the person vaccinated* is equal to marginal cost. Output, however, will be too small, because the amount spent by individuals on vaccination does not fully measure the benefit deriving to *society as a whole*. In other words, marginal utility to society (called marginal social benefit) exceeds marginal cost of production.

External effects are probably quite widespread throughout the economy, although they are difficult to quantify. Moreover, while social benefits can be *greater* than private benefits (as in the case of smallpox vaccinations) they can also be less than private benefits, when expenditure by a private individual reduces, thereby, the satisfaction of someone else. If, for instance, I build a tall house next to yours and block your view, or smoke a cigarette in a confined space you may suffer.

The examples given so far relate to benefits. Equally well, external effects can be on the side of costs. If a business starts a training school for its employees, some trained personnel may leave and work for other businesses, which may profit from lower costs without fully paying for them. If a fish cannery starts up next to a perfumery, the latter may be forced into making special expenditures to prevent fishy smells affecting its perfume.

### Public goods

There is one special case involving external effects which is of great importance. This occurs with what are known as **public goods**, which have marginal social costs approaching zero.

A classical example of a public good is a lighthouse. Once built, the marginal cost of maintenance is very low, and it costs no more to shine for a thousand ships than for a single one. To put the matter in another way, a product may be called a public good if, when one person has more of it, there is no reduction in the quantity available for everyone else. Consider a television programme, which costs as much to put on the air for one viewer as for a million. Compare it with a private good, such as the kipper I had for breakfast. When I ate it, there was nothing edible left for anyone else.

Public goods are sometimes termed **collective consumption** goods to include education, health, defence, etc. We must be careful to distinguish the technical meaning of the term public good from its occasional loose use to describe any goods and services that governments happen to provide.

A freely working price mechanism will not secure the production of the 'right' amount of public goods. Because if marginal cost is zero, then only a zero price is appropriate, and no business will produce goods to give away free. The state may, therefore, decide to intervene, as in the case of goods with some external effects, to encourage or discourage production by means of taxes or subsidies where there are net social benefits or detriments. On the other hand, the government may prefer to deal with the situation by making rules, such as the law that motorists must have insurance to cover third parties who may be hurt through no fault of their own.

There are three major problems to be solved where there are goods for which private and social costs differ.

i. How to quantify the benefits and costs, including all external effects.

ii. To decide whether they should be produced by the state or by private enterprise.

iii. To decide on the best price at which the goods should be sold.

To solve the first problem, elaborate statistical exercises to measure social costs and benefits (known as social cost-benefit analyses) are often undertaken. The second is mainly a political matter, and resembles the problem of whether natural monopolies, dealt with earlier, should be nationalised. The third problem also contains political difficulties. If marginal cost of a public good to the individual is zero, then the only efficient price is also zero—i.e. the products should, perhaps, even be free.

The whole question of the free provision of state services runs into deep political waters, as illustrated by the case of National Health Service charges. If the distribution of income is reasonably satisfactory and the particular goods do mainly benefit users, charging may seem appropriate. But, not infrequently, the government may also be trying to redistribute income in favour of the beneficiaries (e.g. in the case of welfare goods for children, which poor families could not otherwise afford). Charges then might be self-defeating.

## Paternalism

The third set of reasons for being dissatisfied with the distribution of resources that would result from a freely working price mechanism is a good deal easier to understand than either market imperfections or the clash between private and social benefits and costs. We can therefore spend less time on it.

The heading paternalism is used to cover activities of two kinds. The first are those where there may be reason to doubt that consumers are able to judge what is in their own best interest. The second are what are sometimes termed 'non-economic activities'. Paternalism means acting in the capacity of a father. It reasonably applies, therefore, to situations of the first type, where an individual is unable to make the best decisions for himself. For example, a person may not realise that certain kinds of expenditure (e.g. on cigarettes, alcohol, or drugs) may be habit-forming or injurious to health. More generally, we can say that human beings seem to be somewhat myopic. They tend not to pay as much attention to their future as they ought, or at least as they wish they had done later on. Hence, if the state forces people to save, for example, during their working life to provide for a degree of comfort in old age, they may be happier in the long run. Similarly, since the pleasure one can get from reading 'good' books, or hearing 'good' music, cannot necessarily be fully anticipated before the event, the government may decide to subsidise public libraries and the arts.

Strict paternalism probably accounts, too, for at least part of government expenditure on education, since the beneficiaries (the pupils) are not normally the purchasers (the parents) of education services. We may also include under the paternalistic heading those actions of a government which are sometimes described as 'non-economic'. Society, through its government, prohibits certain types of trade which might otherwise be carried on between willing parties. For example, you cannot buy the services of an expert to take your exams for you. Nor can you pay or be paid to commit murder, or deal in slaves. These and other activities are taken out of the market place by governments seeking to provide what we currently believe to be a civilised environment for life. Even defence expenditure is sometimes included in this category, although it might equally well be considered a public good, since defence cannot be provided for one citizen without also being available for another.

## The distribution of income and wealth

The next reason for questioning the allocation of resources under the price mechanism is related to the distribution of income and wealth. Unless we are prepared to accept that the distribution is just and equitable, we may be dissatisfied, not only with the distribution itself, but also with the allocation of resources. For each individual consumer is, in a sense, an elector in the market. He spends his money in one way rather than another, casting his 'votes' for the goods and services he values most highly. The 'votes' are the pounds and pence that he has to spend. However, some people have much more than others, and since tastes are to some extent peculiar both to the individual and also to a person's income level, we may reasonably expect that different distributions of income, and therefore of 'votes', would not be spent in exactly the same way. To take an extreme example, a society with a few very rich people and the remainder very poor might produce mainly bread and luxury goods, like Rolls-Royce cars; while another society where income was equally divided would produce more cheap family cars, meat, and fruit. A glance back at the evidence in Table 1.2 (page 11) can confirm the truth of the general proposition that resource allocation is influenced by income distribution.

We must not fall into the trap of assuming that an unequal distribution of income *must* also be inequitable. For one thing, a person's income is partly derived from his output or productivity. There is, therefore, some basis for regarding the fact that the market rewards the efficient worker more than the inefficient as, to an extent, fair and equitable. More fundamentally, we must be prepared to recognise that any statement about equity is bound to involve value judgments. The only acceptable stand for an economist is to let society judge the merits of its own income distribution, before drawing any conclusions about the efficiency with which the price mechanism allocates resources.

Most people believe that the government should engage in some income redistribution activity. This is attempted in many ways: through progressive taxation, taking a higher proportion of the income of the rich than of the poor; by making transfer payments to the old, the sick, the poor, and the unemployed; by controlling some prices (e.g. certain wages and rents); by providing social services (like health) free to all regardless of whether they can afford them; by interfering in the market place to support the weak against the strong (e.g. by encouraging trade union formation, especially in the nineteenth century).

We need not spend much time asking why the state takes these kinds of action. The simple answer is that it is generally believed that the distribution of income that would result from the free operation of market forces would be grossly unfair. We may recall, from Chapter 5, that the demand for a factor of production depends upon productivity, and that the equilibrium wage determined in the market measures the marginal product of labour. To the extent that a man's income is a function of his ability, it may seem just that he should benefit if he possesses a highly valued skill. At the same time, there is widespread agreement that society does not want the totally disabled, blind, or crippled to starve to death.

Moreover, a person's income may be influenced by age, education, race, and sex; and by the job availabilities of the district in which he lives as well as by the social and psychological pressures to which he is subject (such as those that lead a son towards the occupation of his father). Society is not prepared to allow some of these factors to make a man's income as different from that of another's as the free working of the price mechanism in the factor market might otherwise bring about.

There are two further aspects of the subject of income distribution that must be mentioned. The careful reader will have noticed, the heading of this section is the distribution of income and *wealth*, and that our discussion so far has been about income only. We must acknowledge that a man's wealth, as well as his income, can affect his market 'voting' power. The point is an important one, particularly since wealth in Britain, and in most other countries, is very much more unequally distributed than is income. Indeed, part of the inequality of income distribution may be attributed to the unequal distribution of property, which itself yields income to its owner.

An interesting by-product of this line of thought is worth pursuing briefly. Now that it is admitted that equity in economic terms is not simply a question of income, but also of property distribution, we might wonder if the list really stops there. For example, it has been suggested that equity is really to do with *spending* rather than with earning. An individual's expenditure represents what he takes out of the available pool of goods and services; his income reflects what he puts into it. Therefore, it may be argued, should we perhaps not worry about the highly paid and the wealthy, but only about the big spenders? Moreover, people may be influenced in their view of the justice of allowing some individuals to own great wealth by the manner in which their fortunes were accumulated, e.g., whether as a result of inheritance, thrift, diligence, or good luck.

Here we can do little more than conclude that the idea of equity is many-sided and ambiguous. There are no objective tests which can be of much value. One man's opinion of equity must be set against another's. But we must face the fact that policy decisions are continually made which necessarily imply choosing between different income distributions. We may, for instance, have to make a choice between alternative tax proposals which are said to have the same aim of equity. Suppose we were asked to select the most equitable of the following; an income tax, a wealth tax, an expenditure tax, an inheritance tax, and a capital gains tax. All may be said to aim at making the tax system equitable in some sense or other. We shall not escape making a value judgment in opting for any of them, but we should at least be able to identify a different meaning of equity implied by each.

One other aspect of income distribution must be discussed and then we will come to the fifth and final part of the critique of the operation of the price mechanism in a free market. It relates to the effects of taxation.

So far, we have assumed that the state can, if desired, try to improve the income distribution by, for example, progressive taxation. We must recognise, however, that there may be limits to the power of the state to achieve its aims in this direction; and there may also be costs. High rates of taxation, especially at the margin, may have two important effects. The clearest, perhaps, is that they can lead to tax avoidance and illegal evasion. Some members of the legal and accountancy professions thrive on inventing new ways of keeping tax payments down for clients.

The second, much publicised, effect of high tax rates is that they may lead to lower work effort by individuals. We discussed this question in Chapter 5, without reaching any firm conclusions. Undoubtedly some men have been prompted to work less hard because of taxation, but there are others who have been induced to work harder for the identical reason. Unfortunately, in the present state of economic theory and empirical evidence, it is impossible to judge whether taxation has, on balance, a net incentive or net disincentive effect.

## Time and macroeconomic policy

We should not be surprised to find that time features significantly in the analysis of market failure. The essence of the case for *laissez-faire*, with which we are now familiar, is that economic forces may, in certain conditions, lead to a satisfactory distribution of resources.

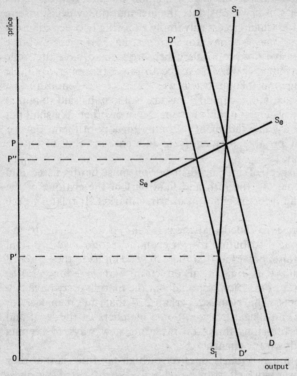

*Figure 8.4* Market price instability. Substantial price fluctuations follow shifts in demand where supply is highly inelastic

But the forces of supply and demand cannot, in the nature of things, act instantaneously. They take time to work. Indeed, we shall find it rewarding to review some of the causes of market failure already discussed in a context in which time is treated as an important consideration. For instance, the longer the time allowed, the easier it is for a firm to enter an industry where a monopoly has been active. Mobility of labour is also greater in the long run than in the short, so that any wage differentials between regions, industries, and even occupations tend to decrease as time passes.

Agriculture is one important area where the price mechanism often functions inadequately because of the time that economic forces take to work. Many agricultural products characteristically operate in conditions both of inelastic demand and of inelastic supply. Demand is not very responsive to price changes for certain basic food-stuffs, such as bread. The same is true of a number of agricultural raw materials because they form a very small part of the total cost of a finished product. (Think, for instance, of the price elasticity of demand for corks by wine importers.) On the supply side, price inelasticity stems often from high storage costs and the existence of a time lag between planting and harvesting. This can be as long as seven years (for a rubber tree), and can lead to low elasticity of supply in response to price changes.

When a market operates in conditions of great inelasticity of supply and demand, there is a tendency for prices to fluctuate substantially with quite small changes in demand. Figure 8.4 illustrates the argument. With an inelastic supply curve, $S_iS_i$, a fall in demand from $DD$ to $D'D'$ leads to a large price fall, from $OP$ to $OP'$, due to the extremely low price elasticities. Compare the smaller price fall following the same change in demand, but with a more elastic supply curve, $S_eS_e$. More important to the farmer than fluctuations in price, however, is the tendency for incomes to oscillate (from low levels in years of bumper crops to high levels when harvests are poor) and which follows from the existence of low elasticity of demand. Governments are, therefore, prone to take steps to help stabilise farm incomes. The chief ways of doing this include the granting of subsidies and the operation of so-called buffer stock schemes, whereby the Government buys or sells a commodity in the open market to offset changes in supply or demand, and thereby reduce the extent of price fluctuations.

Virtually all the examples of market failure discussed so far are connected in one way or another with questions of the allocation and distribution of resources. A further part of the last major area in which the market does not function automatically in the best of all possible ways is concerned rather with macroeconomics, and involves considerations of the level of the total national income, its rate of growth, and the general levels of employment and of prices.

Several deficiencies of the market system in the area of macroeconomics are associated with the time that economic forces take to work. Consider, for instance, the level of unemployment. In the last chapter (see pages 132–34) we saw how the economy could be in a position of equilibrium income at the same time as unemployment was high. This situation has occurred in the past, although full employment has usually been restored *eventually* when a depression has worn itself out. In the period between the two world wars, however, the level of unemployment in Britain never fell below 10 per cent; and, in the nineteenth century, less severe slumps nevertheless kept unemployment high for years.

Almost everyone agrees that prolonged periods of heavy unemployment are undesirable, and to the extent that free markets fail to avoid them, the system must be faulted. Fortunately, since the Second World War economists have understood enough about the working of the economy to be able to propose policies for maintaining full employment. No major depressions have been experienced since that time, although we cannot, of course, ever be sure that the policies have been responsible for the improvement. Moreover, full employment is only one of several macroeconomic goals, and economists have at times been rather less successful in their policy proposals for achieving others.

## Macroeconomic policy objectives

The principal objectives of policy at the macroeconomic level are:

    i. Full employment.
    ii. Stability of the general price level.
    iii. A high rate of economic growth.
    iv. A satisfactory balance of payments position.

Listed in this manner all seem desirable enough aims, but if a rational set of policies is to be devised at the macroeconomic level, we must realise that it may not be possible to pursue all at the same time. We must, therefore, be more precise about each of them.

### Full employment

Full employment is so widely considered to be desirable that any politician who admitted publicly that he did not accept it would be in for a tough time. Yet it is a very imprecise statement of an aim.

How full has employment to be before we can be satisfied that it is 'full'? No one seriously imagines an economy can be efficiently run with every single worker in a job every working day of the year. A certain amount of temporary unemployment is an inevitable price to be paid for progress, as some industries expand and others contract. Moreover, every country has some unemployables who are quite incapable of productive work.

In the light of information of this kind, it seems that it would not be easy to get universal agreement on a precise target in terms of the percentage of the labour force out of work. But why must the target be specified as a percentage? It might be more sensible to set it in terms of the relationship between the number of unemployed and the number of job vacancies. A given per cent unemployed seems much more tolerable if there are more jobs than men seeking work, than if the reverse is the situation. Yet even this kind of target is not without defects. If there are a thousand unemployed steel workers in Swansea, it is not much comfort to know that there are vacancies for the same number of shorthand typists in London.

## Price stability

Consider next the goal of price stability. In contrast to full employment there is no real ambiguity about the objective in this case, although in modern times, with inflationary tendencies dominant, price stability implies simply a general price level that does not increase. Yet absolute stability is rarely achieved because it usually involves sacrificing one or more other policy objectives. It is easier to ensure a low degree of unemployment, for example, if the price level is allowed to rise. Indeed there is some evidence to suggest that there is a direct, though inverse, relationship—sometimes called a **trade-off**—between full employment and price stability. If true, this means that there is a real opportunity cost of having a lower level of unemployment, which may be expressed as a more rapid rate of inflation.

Price stability is, to some extent, less a final objective of policy than is full employment, because the latter is obviously desirable in itself, whereas the case against inflation is less direct and has to be argued. One consequence of rising prices that is widely regarded as unsatisfactory is the tendency for exports to become less competitive, and for the balance of payments to move, therefore, adversely to a country experiencing inflation.[3] The conclusion is dependent upon certain assumptions concerning the nature of supply and demand in international trade, but there is fairly good empirical support for it. However, there are also a number of alternative measures which can

3. More precisely to a country experiencing more rapid inflation than other countries.

help an unfavourable balance on foreign account (see below pp. 169 ff.), and an anti-inflationary policy must be regarded, therefore, as a substitute for the imposition of import restrictions and similar actions.

Inflation is said to be accompanied by certain other regrettable consequences, of which two are particularly important. The first concerns equity, and is based on the proposition that income distribution in an inflationary state is different from that in one where prices are stable. Losers from inflation include persons on incomes which are fixed in money terms, or which at least increase more slowly than the price level; while gainers are those who manage to keep their incomes ahead of rising prices. Creditors also tend to lose relative to debtors.

The difficult question is whether the net effect is inequitable. To answer it we must know the financial circumstances of the individuals affected, and make explicit value judgments about whom we want to gain and to lose. We should also not forget that the longer inflation continues, the more it becomes accepted as a fact of economic life, and the larger the number of people whose incomes are adjusted upwards more or less automatically to keep pace with the price level.

A second important adverse consequence attributed to inflation is its tendency to reduce the efficiency with which the price mechanism allocates resources. When the general price level is stable, one can quickly identify the sectors where prices are rising and those where they are falling. Factors of production can move between sectors, attracted by rising prices which reflect changes in underlying supply or demand conditions. But if the majority of prices are tending upwards, factor movements have to respond to *relative* price changes, and it is much more difficult to identify those which are rising relatively rapidly. Moreover, in periods of extended inflation, it may be virtually impossible to know how much things which take a long time to make, such as ships, will really cost when they have been completed. And, in the general uncertainty about future levels of costs and prices, wastefulness and inefficiency can appear quite unimportant. Inflation tends also to stimulate expenditure on speculative items, such as jewellery and paintings rather than on productive investments, as individuals search for safe repositories for their savings as hedges against the rising price level. Finally, inflation may reduce the incentive for individuals to save in order to provide for old age, against ill-health, etc.

One of the strongest arguments in the case against inflation is bound up with preventing its developing into the runaway form known as hyper-inflation, when prices can jump substantially between the time a worker does a job and the time he is paid for it. Hyper-inflation is fortunately rare enough; but if the pace of inflation accelerates continually, loss of confidence in the currency can result. People lose faith in money and resort to barter, hoarding commodities and money substitutes, such as cigarettes, instead of currency. Complete collapse of the price mechanism and major breakdown of a country's economy may ensue, calling for the most drastic measures before confidence in a new currency can be established.

## Economic growth

There is a superficial similarity between the policy goal of economic growth, implying a rise in national income, and that of full employment. In each case, there is an implication that the sky is, as it were, the desired limit, provided only that there is no sacrifice in the achievement of any other goals. The implication can, however, be misleading. Economic growth is not wanted for its own sake, but in order that living standards can be raised.

One of the simplest ways of raising future living standards is to increase the amount of current investment, which involves, in turn, relatively lower current consumption. Hence, there is an obvious dilemma, or choice, between raising either current or future living standards, i.e. between generations. It should be realised, too, that economic growth may be achieved if people take less leisure and work longer hours. But no one supposes that the result is necessarily desirable.

The argument suggests, therefore, that we cannot conclude that the higher the rate of growth of the economy, the better off the people will be. The nation has a choice of growth rates and development patterns, and the government has the political task of choosing between them. The state may of course take notice of the signs provided by market forces here. The price of labour in the factor market, for instance, is a measure of the loss of satisfaction that a worker suffers at the margin for the 'last' hour worked. In competitive conditions this must be true, or he would be better off if he chose to work a different number of hours, either more or less.

The rate of interest, too, provides some guidance on how much people are prepared to sacrifice present for future consumption. Interest, it will be recalled, is paid for saving, or not consuming. Hence, at the margin, it measures the loss of satisfaction that people suffer when consumption is reduced. If they do not consider worthwhile the higher future living standards that they hope will follow, they will tend to save less (and vice versa). The market is, however, very poorly equipped to solve, on its own, the problem of the most desirable growth rate. External effects are present, and there are major information gaps, because growth involves the unknowable future, and the private individual is in a weak position to make important judgments about it.

Moreover, the market rate of interest is liable to fluctuate in the short run for quite irrelevant technical reasons which have nothing to do with the community's idea of the most desirable growth rate. The government usually steps in, therefore, to fix a target growth rate, having regard to the costs and benefits likely to accrue over time at different rates. Setting the target is one of the state's most important tasks, particularly since the achievement of a high rate of economic growth has become one of the symbols of successful government. The reasons for this fairly recent conventional wisdom are beyond the scope of an introductory book on economics. But international comparisons of growth rates are often made, and no government wants to find itself near the bottom of the 'league table'. We can only note here that the choice of a target growth rate involves political considerations and, therefore, value judgments.

Regulating the growth rate is not only an important task for government; it is also a very difficult one. This is partly because of conflicts with other goals, especially price stability, and also because we are not sure exactly what really causes economic growth in the first place. It is easy enough to say that real national income may rise more rapidly the larger is the supply of factors of production, the more efficiently they are used, and the greater the rate of technological advance. But it is a great deal harder to find out how to control each of these determinants.

How, for instance, can the supply of factors be increased? What are the roles of education and research in raising the rate of technological advance? How does one induce managers to operate more efficiently? We only have rough ideas of the answers to these questions, which lie to some extent at least, in the realm of microeconomics.[5] Much of our earlier discussion of the part played by market imperfections as causes of market failure is clearly relevant to the question of how to control growth rates. But there is little more by way of useful conclusions to be drawn from the discussion, save perhaps that macroeconomics and microeconomics are not entirely separate branches of the discipline we are studying.

## A satisfactory balance of payments

This, the last objective of economic policy to be dealt with is, perhaps, the least inherently desirable of all. A satisfactory balance of payments is wanted largely because its absence tends to inhibit economic growth and to make full employment, and sometimes other goals, more difficult to attain. Economic growth has, for instance, been inhibited in Britain in recent years by a tendency for imports to rise when national income rises, causing thereby a strain on the balance of payments.

It is necessary to point out that the word 'satisfactory' in the stated objective does not necessarily mean 'as favourable as possible'. No country wishes to receive, perpetually, more than it pays out, unless it wants to make continuous loans to foreigners. Even then, unless foreigners want to go on accepting loans, other countries will be in unfavourable positions on their balances of payments. Foreigners will be forced, eventually, to take corrective action by restricting their imports, for example, which will hardly please the first country very much.

There is, therefore, something of a problem to decide what should properly be meant by a satisfactory balance of payments. As a first approximation, we may make use of the now familiar concept of equilibrium. The balance of payments may be described as being in equilibrium if the demand for and supply of foreign currencies are equal. There is then no tendency for a country to lose (or gain) reserves of gold (or foreign currencies), and the rate of exchange has no tendency to rise or to fall.

However, as we know, supply and demand do not work in a vacuum, but within the influence of a social and institutional framework. We cannot simply interpret the word 'satisfactory' for the balance of payments to mean 'in a state of equilibrium' without regard to the underlying influences. The balance of payments may, for instance, be in equilibrium at one growth rate for the economy and yet unsatisfactory at a higher growth rate, which induces a loss of reserves. Or, to take another example, at one distribution of income within a country, the balance of payments may be apparently sound, whereas a redistribution from rich to poor could, perhaps, result in a rise in imports which would change the situation entirely. Again, and not uncommonly in the past, the balance of payments may be kept in a state of equilibrium by the existence of a level of unemployment that is regarded as intolerable. These illustrations serve only to emphasise the interrelationship between the balance of payments and other basic policy goals.

A country whose balance of payments is under pressure is faced with a number of alternative policies from which to choose.

i. *Use up reserves of gold and foreign currencies.* This is obviously a short-run solution only. When the reserves are exhausted another policy will be needed.

ii. *Obtain loans from other countries.* This is another short-run solution. Both (i) and (ii) are, however, often useful as they give a country time to make fundamental but essential changes in the structure of its economy in order to strengthen its long-run balance of payments —e.g. to increase the efficiency of its export industries or to reduce its dependence on imported raw materials.

iii. *Restrict imports.* There are several ways of cutting expenditure on imported goods. We mention some of the most common techniques. Import quotas may be imposed, limiting the quantity allowed into the country; tariffs may be levied raising the price of imports; subsidies may be given to domestic producers of import substitutes; expenditure on invisible imports may be restricted (e.g. through foreign travel allowances).

iv. *Stimulate exports.* It is not usually as easy to stimulate exports as it is to control imports, but subsidies may, for example, be offered to firms which increase the value of their exports.

v. *Alter the exchange rate.* Devaluation (lowering the exchange rate) tends to reduce the foreign price of exports and to raise the domestic price of imports. It may, therefore, improve the balance of payments, although if demands are not sufficiently responsive to price changes, upward valuation should normally be more successful. A highly controversial question is whether it is preferable to alter the exchange rate in stages (the so-called adjustable, or crawling, peg), or to allow complete freedom for the rate to move up and down with changes in supply and demand. The issue hangs partly upon whether speculation ensues, which causes wider fluctuations in the rate of exchange under one system or under the other. We cannot go further into the matter here.

vi. *Deflate.* The final remedy for a country which is aiming at an improvement in its balance of payments is to use fiscal and monetary **deflationary** policies to bring downward pressure on the national income. Deflation works by restraining the growth of income and also, therefore, of the demand for imports, while it may also encourage exports. It is not, however, a solution which commends itself to a nation with a high level of unemployment.

For a country in a state of boom, on the other hand, a slowing down of the growth rate may not appear so unsatisfactory, since it may also help to reduce inflationary pressure. Restrictive policy in such circumstances is even given the more polite title **disinflation**. We may note that deflation (or disinflation) frequently involves a rise in the rate of interest which may provide additional support for the exchange rate by encouraging foreign loans into a country and so relieving pressure on the capital account, at least in the short run.

## Policy choices

It may have occurred to the reader that the solution chosen from the list of alternative policies available to a country in balance of payments difficulties has vital implications for other countries besides the one taking action. Nations are economically interdependent in a way which resembles to some extent the results of external, or spillover, effects discussed earlier in this chapter. Not surprisingly, therefore, some supra-national government institutions have been set up, with rules designed to reduce the propensity for countries to adapt 'beggar-my-neighbour' policies which benefit none in the end. Examples are the International Monetary Fund, which exercises control over the exchange rate policies of member countries, and GATT (the General Agreement on Tariffs and Trade) which performs a similar function with regard to import restrictions and export subsidies.

## Conflicts in policy goals

The whole question of deciding on the appropriate set of economic policies for government bristles with difficulties. Certainly, we should all prefer a cheap policy to an expensive one; and a cure for a recognised ill rather than a palliative. These are, however, small matters that we cannot attempt to evaluate here. But drawing upon some of the examples discussed in this chapter so far, we may be able to get certain issues in perspective.

The most basic issue of all is that there are several desirable

**goals** of economic policy and it is inevitable that they should, at times, conflict. The second point is that there is, almost always, a choice of techniques, or **instruments** as they are sometimes called, available for achieving any given goal. Thirdly, and this is an aspect of policy that has, perhaps, not been sufficiently stressed, the extent to which goals conflict depends upon the techniques which are chosen to achieve them.

Let us take a simple example. Suppose it is desired to stimulate saving in order to promote economic growth. We can consider two of many alternative ways of trying to achieve this objective. One might be to *reduce* the rate of income tax on the rich. Another could be to *increase* it, with the intention of increasing government saving. Of course, neither policy might succeed. But if they did, each would be likely to have a different effect on income distribution. And, if society's value judgments about equity were in favour of a more equal distribution of income, then the second policy would *ceteris paribus*, be the preferable one.

Other examples of the way in which the likelihood of conflicts is affected by the choice of policy instruments have been mentioned earlier. Take, for instance, the case of a country in balance of payments difficulties which is also experiencing inflationary pressure. Consider, again, two alternative policy instruments—devaluation and deflation—for dealing with the balance of payments. We assume both would be successful. But the former will tend to increase inflation as import prices rise and exports are stimulated. Deflation, on the other hand, would tend to reduce inflationary pressure as well as help the balance of payments.

Here again, of course, we must stipulate other things remain equal, since deflation might inhibit the successful achievements of other goals, such as full employment and an equitable distribution of income. The argument ought to be taken one stage further. We cannot assume that a government is faced with alternative policy instruments, each of which can achieve a given goal, and that all we need to do is to select the best for each occasion after considering all possible side effects. Frankly, we cannot claim that economists fully understand exactly how each technique works in practice. So our choice is rather different, and not nearly so clear cut.

The issue may be illustrated by reference to one of the most controversial policy problems of recent years. Consider the macroeconomic policy goal of short-run stabilisation, i.e. of smoothing out the cyclical ups and downs of national income. How best can one keep the time paths of income and prices steady?

There are three main instruments to choose from—monetary policy, fiscal policy, and incomes policy. The supporters of monetary policy claim that the best technique is to adjust the supply of money (and perhaps interest rates) restricting or releasing credit as booms or slumps appear to be getting out of hand. The supporters of fiscal policy prefer budgetary changes, with a government surplus (or deficit) when the private sector is tending towards inflation (or deflation). Those who favour an incomes policy argue for institutional arrangements to keep income rises roughly in line with productivity changes.

It is obviously important to know why even experts differ quite profoundly on a matter like this. There are three main reasons. First, there are clear political implications in choosing between the various techniques. We cannot go into them further than to mention that the use of each technique probably has a different effect on the distribution of income. Second, there are problems of implementation, questions of cost, of the availability of information, and of timing. We would naturally prefer a fast and cheap policy instrument to a slow, expensive one, but there is no certainty that one policy is better than others on both of these counts.

Finally, and most significant, economists may differ because they have their own opinions about how the policies work in practice. Hence, we should not even be surprised if the experts change their views on what constitutes the best approach. A fiscal policy supporter might, for instance, switch allegiance to monetary policy if he became convinced that budgetary changes could never be made quickly enough to prevent cyclical swings up and down. The fundamental problem is that economists still do not understand enough of the way the economy functions. The moral is clear enough. More positive economics to improve knowledge and more power to control the economy.

## Comparative economic systems

Economic policy has been discussed in this chapter in as detached and objective a manner as possible. It should be emphasised, however, that any writings on this subject are liable to be influenced by the personal opinions of the author. There is no better way to appreciate the significance of this remark than to read carefully the sections on policy in other textbooks and to try to identify sources of bias. The most conscientious writer cannot avoid them entirely.

Taking the broadest possible view, much of the argument about economic policy boils down to a basic political viewpoint, whether one is attracted more by *laissez-faire* or by planning. Those who see greater virtues in a freely working price mechanism stress the advantages it confers. Self-interest supplants government. The market is cheap and impersonal. Price is the same for every person who enters the market, regardless of sex, colour, race, or religious belief. The price mechanism works continuously, reflecting changes in supply or demand, while planning decisions take time to be put into effect. Moreover, the ballot box provides only an infrequent opportunity for consumers to express approval or disapproval of what the planners have achieved.

On the other hand, those who see the greater virtue in planning and favour state intervention, stress rather the past record of unemployment under *laissez-faire*, the desirability of redistributing income, the prevalence of monopoly, and the divergences between private and social costs which result in an imbalance between private and public sectors, typified by too many motor cars and too large classes in the schoolrooms.

There are obvious weaknesses on both sides. No one can seriously believe that 100 per cent *laissez-faire* or 100 per cent central planning is ideal for an economy. As we have shown, the case for some kind of government intervention is different from, and stronger than, the case for central planning itself. Indeed, it is remarkable how, in recent years, central planners in some Communist countries have come to realise that prices can play an important role in a socialist state, without private ownership of the means of production.

At the same time, economists in the West have increasingly come to accept the existence of deficiencies in the market system, and have begun to experiment with techniques such as that known as 'indicative planning', whereby the government prepares a moderately detailed outline plan for the economy, which may make business forecasting in the private sector simpler. When two traditionally opposing beliefs begin to move closer together, there's probably a moral to be drawn somewhere. We may wonder what it is.

Chapter 9

# The Methods of Economics—
# Tools and Techniques

---

We have almost reached the end of this introductory book on economics without devoting any space to a formal statement of what economics is about and what methods are used by economists. This may strike the reader as a trifle odd. It is certainly unusual for a textbook not to deal with 'scope and method' early on.

Experience suggests that students are bored by spending a lot of time mastering the tools of the trade early in their studies. They are better put straight to work; to learn by doing. We have, however, now acquired enough of the flavour of the subject to ask intelligently the questions; what is the nature of economics? and what are its main elementary techniques of analysis?

## The social sciences

The speed at which any subject advances is closely related to that at which useful new ideas can be generated. Each group of subjects tends to develop methods for its own encouragement. Economics belongs to the group known as the social sciences, which includes sociology, political science, and social psychology. All have two important characteristics in common. They are 'social' and they are 'scientific'.

i. *'Social'*. Their subject matter is human society. The social sciences, taken together, are concerned with the explanation of human behaviour, past, present, and future. Their job would be complete, as it never will be, if all future human actions could be predicted with certainty.

There is no point in enquiring too closely into the exact borders between the different social sciences. For one thing they are not eternal constants. As the analysis of one aspect of behaviour becomes more fully developed, there is a tendency for it to break off and become a separate subject. Today, sociology and political science are regarded as distinctive disciplines, whereas a few decades ago they were studied, together with economics, in what was called 'political economy'.

A second reason for not trying to define the subject matter of each social science is that it cannot be done precisely anyway. It used to be the fashion in textbooks to consider the merits of alternative definitions of economics. But the only faultless statement ever reached is the uninformative 'economics is what economists do', so that the matter no longer seems worth discussing.

There are a great many areas of overlap between one social science and another, as there are between say, physics and chemistry. It may be helpful to learn that economists are concerned with questions relating to the production and consumption of goods and services, rather than with the development of moral values. Yet this vague kind of statement may be misleading. Both sociologists and psychologists would claim an interest in many of the same areas of social behaviour as economists.

To take an example, production depends on productivity—and therefore on how hard people work. This in turn depends, among other things, on the form of social organisation in factories, which is a subject for sociologists. More than one social science may, therefore, be able to contribute to the understanding of social behaviour. Even when it comes to predicting so obviously economic a matter as the future level of output of goods and services, for instance, it is obvious that economists working alone would be likely to do a poorer job than if they could call upon the work of other social scientists, who might throw light on such matters as the number of days that may be lost from strikes or the chances of a change in the political colour of the government. We must not, however, be discouraged by the fact that social scientists do not know how to predict these and other aspects of social behaviour with a high degree of certainty. The subjects are young and developing fast.

ii. *'Scientific'*. Beginning students used to debate questions like whether economics is as scientific a subject as physics or chemistry, but the topic is no more fruitful than comparing alternative definitions of economics. The main point to be made about a scientific approach is that it involves confronting theories with evidence before incorporating them into the main body of learning. The method contrasts with one which involves emotions and impressions, and which may be labelled unscientific. There is no reason to use the term unscientific in a pejorative sense. There simply is no scientific way of judging whether Laurence Olivier is a cleverer actor than Richard Burton or whether Shakespeare was a better author than Tolstoy. These issues are no less interesting, although there does not appear to be an objective means of assembling evidence about them, and no way of coming to a conclusion, other than by assembling impressions.

In economics, in contrast, there is plenty of scope for comparing theories with facts. Chapter 1 opened with a discussion of family budgets, and a theory was advanced that high housing expenditure in London was attributable to high incomes there. We then examined statistics of household expenditure, to see whether they did or did not support the theory. We were, in a very rudimentary way, checking a hypothesis against the facts. To the extent that economics proceeds in this manner it is valid to describe the subject as being a science.

## A framework for analysis

We shall return later to deal with the techniques by which theories may be tested, but it will be useful, first, to suggest briefly the outline of a procedure for dealing with an economic problem; such as that involved in predicting future output in the economy.

*Step 1. Identify the problem precisely.* The problem should be stated in a form that we can, in principle, hope to find facts which may relate to it. For example, there is no point in asking generally what the future output of the economy will be. We must specify, say, total output; or the output of an identifiable category of goods or services such as whisky or baked beans. If we use a general category, such as capital goods or consumer goods, we must state exactly what is included under those somewhat ambiguous headings. Finally, and no less important, we must identify the precise period of time with which we are concerned, i.e. a particular year, the first quarter of a year, etc.

*Step 2. Put forward a possible explanation of the event under consideration.* The next step is to consider carefully and state precisely all potential causes of the event under consideration after rejecting all but the strictly relevant. Suppose, for instance, we want to forecast the output of consumption goods next year. We may decide that it depends chiefly on how much the population wants to spend on consumption goods, which in turn depends on total income. If we can establish the relationship in a *quantitative* form, such as the following: 'Consumption next year depends on income next year, and 75 per cent of income is on average always spent on consumption goods'; and if we know also that income next year will be £40 million, then we have a precisely quantified theory expressed in a manner which may be tested against the fact of what really happens next year.

*Step 3. Assemble factual evidence relevant to the problem*. The final step in the procedure is concerned with checking the value of the previous analysis by examining whether it helps to explain economic events in the real world. The most obvious way of checking a statement (that made above about next year's consumption, for example) is, of course, to wait until next year and see if it turns out to be correct. However, there is no need to wait so long before testing the hypothesis that consumption expenditure is 75 per cent of the year's income. If the theory is a general one (and to be continually useful it must be so), it should have been true last year and in previous years as well. We can, therefore, assemble evidence (or data, as the facts are sometimes called) from the past history of both income and consumption. From the former we can calculate a set of **expected** (or predicted) consumption figures by taking always 75 per cent of income. If we then compare figures of expected consumption with the actual or **observed** values, we have performed a test of the theory. If the observed and expected values are usually close together, we may provisionally accept the hypothesis as useful. If they are far apart, it should be treated as at least unproven, and of little value for predicting the future.

The three steps outlined above represent what may be called a scientific approach to the analysis of an economic event. Do not be put off by someone who tells you it is not scientific because theories in economics do not always apply with certainty to every situation. The essence of a scientific approach consists in the confrontation of fact and theory. We may recognise that some established relationships in the 'pure' sciences hold more securely than in the social sciences, though this does not make them any more scientific. We shall return to consider reasons behind this shortly.

### Branches of economics

Economics has traditionally been subdivided into a number of different branches.

i. *Microeconomics* and *macroeconomics*. This distinction (which was mentioned in Chapter 6, p. 100) is partly suggested by the words themselves—*micro* implying a close look at each part of the economy; *macro* implying a broader perspective, allowing one to view the economy as a whole, ignoring the detail of its constituent parts.

More generally, microeconomics is concerned with questions of resource allocation, involving the analysis of supply, demand, and price formation. Macroeconomics, in contrast, deals with such matters as the determinants of the level of national income, the volume of total employment, the average general level of prices, and other aspects of *aggregate* economic behaviour. As we now know, some specialised techniques have been developed in each of these subject areas. But there is a considerable overlap between microeconomics and macroeconomics, and the distinction should not be exaggerated. A full understanding of economic behaviour necessarily involves both of them.

ii. *Theoretical economics and applied economics.* This distinction corresponds broadly to that between our Steps 2 and 3 described above—namely between the formulation and the testing of theories. We may note here a possible implication that theories come *first*, and testing *afterwards*. Such a method is known as a **deductive** one. It is to be contrasted with an **inductive** method, where the facts to be explained are examined first, and a theory then designed to fit them.[1] Both methods are used in the physical sciences. An example of inductive reasoning could be the theories offered to account for newly observed phenomena like pulse stars. An example of deductive methods could be those which led physicists to predict the existence of new elements *before* they were observed.

The approach of modern economics does not really fit into either category. Current work in the subject is concerned with analysing the same kinds of phenomena that have long interested economists—e.g. the prediction of consumption expenditure. It often succeeds after an examination of the reasons why previous theories proved deficient in explaining events. We cannot, therefore, aptly describe the method as being strictly inductive or deductive.

iii. *Economic principles and economic policy.* We now draw attention to a particularly important distinction in the subject matter of economics—that between economic principles and economic policy. By principles we mean those parts of economic theory which are, for one reason or another, accepted as the best available analysis of economic behaviour—i.e. we are using word 'principles' to cover both Steps 2 and 3 of our method. What remains is a branch of the

1. An alternative distinction, between descriptive and analytical economics, might imply this opposite ordering—i.e. description of the economy first, with analysis later.

subject which has so far been left out of the discussion, and which concerns those economic matters which cannot be settled, even in principle, by referring to facts, because these matters involve making moral decisions, or **value judgments.** Questions such as whether the level of income tax is too high, or the rate of economic growth is too low are of this kind. They are known in economics as **normative** statements, to distinguish them those those of a **positive** kind—statements such as whether a rise in income tax will increase or decrease hours worked by labour, or what effect a lowering of interest rates will have on the level of investment.

The distinguishing characteristic of all these positive questions is that economists can offer answers to them which can, in principle, be

(i)

(ii)

*Figure 9.1*

tested against evidence. Positive statements, however, cannot lead to *policy* conclusions. Somebody must make a decision about the *desirability* of, say, increasing the hours worked by labour or economic growth before an answer can be given to normative questions, such as whether the income tax is too high. Only then can one begin to think about deciding whether income tax is too high or too low.

The economist acting in his professional role (or, to use the latin jargon commonly employed, '*qua* economist') is not entitled to make such value judgments. As a citizen, of course, he has every right to do so, but it is thought best to keep economics as *value free* as possible by leaving value judgments to be decided by politicians. The job of the economist in government, for example, should not include setting policy objectives. It should be limited to offering advice about the ways in which a given policy might be achieved. If, for example, the government wished to lower the level of unemployment, the economist might inspect the theories which try to explain the causes of unemployment and propose alternative means of achieving the given objective, setting out where possible the probable effects of adopting each on the economy.

It would be misleading to leave the topic of value judgments in economic policy with the idea that these can always be isolated, and the economist left with only positive objective questions. A purely objective assessment of an event implies that it must be approached from all possible viewpoints and without preconceived prejudices. Yet we are innately incapable of doing this, because we have limited capabilities as individuals.

Take for example the well-known puzzle picture in Figure 9.1. Suppose we ask the apparently objective question, how many cubes are there in the picture? The question might seem to be a positive one which can be settled by appealing to the facts. Yet there are two equally correct answers. If you were looking for cubes like (i) the answer is ten. If you were counting those like (ii) it is twelve. There is clearly no reason for preferring one answer to another, unless we know in advance that there is more than one way of looking at the picture. We cannot conclude that either is correct simply because it accords exactly with the facts as we happen to see them.

The social sciences suffer particularly severely from the kind of biases which are reflected in our individual ways of looking at problems, mainly because the world is such a complicated place that we cannot possibly see everything in perspective at the same time. We are, moreover, prisoners of our own environment from the moment we are born. There can be few better ways of bringing this truth home than by comparing a number of science fiction novels written at different times. It is quite startling how quickly they appear 'dated', not so much because of technical developments as because of the idiom in which they are written. The same difficulty of escaping from environmental influences applies also in economics. A statistical table can suggest different hypotheses to each of several economists, depending on their backgrounds and education.

If you want to make an experiment, show the top seven lines of Figure I. 1 in Chapter 1 (page 15,) to a few friends with different training and ask them to summarise it for you in their own words. It is a fair bet that someone who had never been exposed to economics would not refer to prices or incomes. Yet an economist is almost certain to think about these factors and mention these words in his summary. An economist cannot completely escape the need to make a selection from all conceivable hypotheses in interpreting the nature of an economic event, even when he does his best to be objective.

We must not be too discouraged by the argument of this section. While the implication that economists are both fallible and incapable of pure objectivity is true, at the same time we may draw the conclusion that a new idea or theory may turn out to derive simply from a novel way of looking at an old set of data.

### Economic analysis—model building

When an economist sets to work on a problem he begins by constructing what is called a **model**, describing the event which he wishes to explain and the main factors which are causally related to it. Any model contains the following elements:

i. A **dependent variable**—the event to be explained.

ii. One or more **independent** predictors or **variables**—the factors that determine the behaviour of the dependent variable.

iii. **Behavioural assumptions,** the nature of the causal relationships between explanatory and dependent variables.

For example, in Chapter 4 we used what we may now recognise as a model to analyse the demand for ice cream. The dependent variable was the quantity of ice cream demanded per unit of time; the independent variable was the price of ice cream; and the behavioural assumptions included the hypothesis that consumers always tried to maximise their satisfaction in deciding how many ice creams to buy.

### Abstractions

The reason why the economist starts with a simplified model of an economy is that the world is a very complex place, and he cannot hope to incorporate all the explanatory variables which could possibly influence the behaviour of the dependent variable in his analysis. This means that it is necessary to concentrate deliberately on the main determinants in an attempt to establish the relationship between each of them and the dependent variable.

This process of omitting certain explanatory factors is called abstraction. There are several bases for selecting dependent variables for exclusion from the model. One is that they are thought to be of minor importance. The price of wafer biscuits, for instance, could conceivably influence the demand for ice cream, but it is unlikely to be important quantitatively. A second reason for excluding a predictor variable is that there is no likelihood of obtaining reliable information about it. The weather is a good example here, in so far as it influences the demand for ice cream. But we are unlikely to be able to predict it with a high degree of accuracy for any particular week in the future because a week is too short a period to be able to do so.

The most common reason for excluding an explanatory variable from a model is because it is improbable that there will be any significant change in the relationship between it and the dependent variable during the period of time for which the model is constructed. Thus the influence of the level of consumers' income and tastes may not be expected to change when we examine the relationship between the price of ice creams and the demand for them in the short run. We therefore make the assumption that these factors are unchanged over the period, 'other things remaining equal' (*ceteris paribus*).

It can hardly be over-emphasised that the usefulness of an economic model in explaining events in the real world depends upon how realistic the assumptions are. If our model of the demand for ice cream were used to predict behaviour over a period when tastes did change significantly, it would not, of course, give results that were of much value. Applicability is the acid test, and the model builder's task is to bear this in mind while maintaining a model of manageable proportions. If the model fails on test, a new and better one is called for. We return to this point later.

*Causal relationships*

Having excluded certain possible explanatory factors from the model, we are left with a number of predictor variables and a dependent variable. The next step is to specify the precise nature of the relationship between them. This involves a statement of the **sign** of the relationship and of its **form**.

The term sign is borrowed from the language of mathematics, and can be either positive or negative. For example, the price of ice cream is said to be negatively related to demand if a rise or fall in price leads to a change in the opposite (inverse) direction in quantity demanded. If, however, price and quantity always moved in the same direction (up or down together), the sign would be positive.

The form of the relationship between a dependent and an independent variable describes more or less exactly how the one depends on the other. For instance, the demand for ice cream might be specified as being determined by the price of ice cream in many different ways, e.g.:

i. Quantity demanded is (inversely) proportionate to price; i.e. if price rises by $x$ per cent, demand falls by $y$ per cent.

ii. Quantity demanded is (inversely) proportionate to price when price is higher than a specific level.

iii. Quantity demanded is (inversely) related to the square root of the price of ice cream.

We should always adopt the form of the model which seems to be most realistic. Later we should test it by confronting it with evidence about behaviour in the real world.

It should be noted, incidentally, that the model is expressed verbally. Economists commonly employ two other ways of specifying models—graphical and algebraic. We shall deal with the latter later in the chapter, but graphical methods have been used several times throughout this book. We have therefore relegated the section explaining the meaning and use of graphs to an appendix (see page 207 ff). If you are in any doubt about graphical methods, you should refer to this section before reading further.[1]

## Equilibrium models

In leading up to the treatment of algebraic methods we must now draw attention to an important feature of the model of the demand for ice cream used for purposes of illustration above. The model contains only a single behavioural relationship between two variables. By itself it can determine the quantity demanded only if we make assumptions about price. In other words, for every value which we ascribe to the price of ice cream, our model can forecast the quantity of ice cream demanded.

The model would be much more useful if it could predict not only the demand, but also the price of ice cream. This would be more likely if we specified that the price of ice cream was determined by the requirement that the quantity demanded should equal the quantity supplied. However, there would still be one exclusion from the model

1. Mathematical methods are also the subject of a special volume in this series: *Mathematics for Modern Economics,* by R. Morley.

which would prevent it predicting price and quantity, because we have added a new variable, quantity supplied, without stating what supply itself depends on.

We may draw on our knowledge of the nature of market forces (especially from Chapter 4) to add a relationship to fill this gap—that quantity supplied depends on market price. Consider then the nature of our new model. It contains three variables, demand, supply, and price, which are *interdependent*. We now have to examine sets of relationships between price and quantity demanded, and between price and quantity supplied, until we find that price at which the quantities demanded and supplied are equal. Such a model is said to be 'solved' when we have found that price. Any 'solution' must, in other words, be one which satisfies all the specifications of the model, which we refer to here as an 'equilibrium model', because it contains interrelationships between the variables.

Let us take a simple non-economic example of a model in which there is the same kind of interdependence as in our model of market price and quantity. Suppose we have a stock of marbles and two boys, Adam and Bill. The boys can take marbles subject to assumptions about their behaviour stipulated by the model, which are:

i. Adam must always have twice as many marbles as Bill.

ii. Bill must have 21 marbles if Adam does not have any at all. But for every marble Adam has, Bill's total is reduced by 3 (i.e. Bill has 21 marbles minus 3 times the number owned by Adam).

This model contains interdependence because Adam's marbles depend on how many Bill has, and vice versa. Because of this interdependence, there are not a variety of different numbers of marbles for Adam which are consistent with numbers for Bill. In other words, there are not several *solutions* to the model, but in this case, only a single one. For instance, if Adam has 2 marbles Bill should have 1 to satisfy Condition (i) in the model, but Bill should have 15 to satisfy Condition (ii). If Bill has 9 marbles, Adam should have 18 to satisfy Condition (i), but only 4 to satisfy Condition (ii).

The only mutually consistent solution to the model for both Adam and Bill, and which satisfies both Conditions (i) and (ii), is for Adam to have 6 and Bill to have 3. Such a solution for an economic model is called a *state of equilibrium*. It implies that there are values ascribed to each of the variables which are consistent with each other, and which do not prevent any of the behavioural hypotheses of the model from being realised.

The values of the variables (the number of marbles for Adam and

Bill) in equilibrium, can be found by experimenting, as we have done by trial and error with different numbers. Alternatively if we put the model into graphical form, we can also quickly find the solution. In Figure 9.2 we measure Adam's marbles on the vertical and Bill's on the horizontal axis. The line marked Adam then shows Condition (i). It is drawn as follows. Assume Bill has any number, say 5, marbles, Adam must then have 10, so $\alpha'$ is one point on the line. Next assume Bill has any other number, say 4. Then Adam must have 8, giving

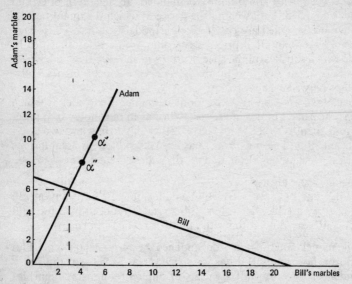

*Figure 9.2*

point $\alpha''$ on the graph. All we have to do next is to draw a line through $\alpha'$ and $\alpha''$ to give the line marked Adam. In a similar way, the line marked Bill can be drawn to give all values which satisfy Condition (ii).[2]

We can see that the only numbers of marbles for Adam and Bill that are mutually consistent are those indicated by the point of intersection of the two lines. Dropping perpendiculars to the two axes, we read off values of 6 marbles for Adam and 3 for Bill.

Let us now use the same technique to solve an economic equilibrium model, of the kind which we have used on several occasions in this book, for the determination of the equilibrium of supply and

2. See Appendix, pages 207 ff., for details of how to construct a graph.

demand in a single market. We specify the behavioural relationships as follows:

i. The number of houses consumers wish to purchase (demand) is inversely related to their price.

ii. The number of houses producers wish to supply (supply) is positively related to their price.

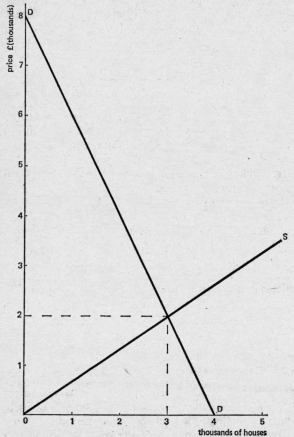

*Figure 9.3*

If we now give precise values to the relationships, we can find the equilibrium price and quantity for the two conditions to be satisfied simultaneously—let them be:

   i. Demand is always 4,000 minus half the price of houses.
   ii. Supply is always $1\frac{1}{2}$ times the price of houses.

Plotting the demand and supply lines graphically, we get Figure 9.3, which gives as the solution a price of £2,000 and a quantity of 3,000 houses. In other words, if the behavioural assumptions of the model are correct, the only possible equilibrium price for houses is £2,000; and 3,000 houses is the only quantity that can be bought and sold without leaving at least some unsatisfied producers or consumers. This is the 'solution' to the equilibrium model.

### Making a model work

A model which describes an economic system which has a solution[3] can, however, do more than indicate a relationship (e.g. that between the equilibrium price and quantity in a market as in the case above). The model can be *operated*, or made to work; that is to say it can deal with a *change* in one or more of the variables, and describe the new equilibrium conditions to which the values will tend.

Suppose, for example, the supply and demand conditions of our last model were originally as portrayed in Figure 9.3, but for some reason outside the model (termed **exogenous** to it) demand conditions change. A spontaneous change in tastes might make consumers wish to buy 2,000 fewer houses at every price. A new demand curve would then be needed—that represented by the line $D'D'$ in Figure 9.4. We can easily see that the new equilibrium price and quantity would be at the intersection of the supply curve $OS$, and the new demand curve $D'D'$. Our model has been worked to show that a decrease in demand of 2,000 houses (at every price) leads to a fall in price from £2,000 to £1,000, and a reduction in the quantity bought (and sold) from 3,000 to 1,500.

### The role of time in economic models

In the main text of this book we frequently made reference to the importance of stipulating the time allowed for economic forces to work. Accordingly we distinguished between short-period and long-period effects. Similarly we must specify the time periods in our formal models.

3. Many models may have several 'solutions', e.g. if one or more of the behavioural relationships specified by it are non-linear. We are not however (much) concerned with them in this book.

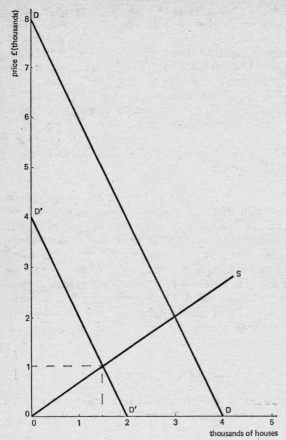

*Figure 9.4*

In addition we must take account of two other aspects of the importance of time.

i. *Dynamics*. Sometimes equilibrium may never be reached in a market because the process of moving towards it sets up new forces which 'feed back' on each other and continually disturb any tendency towards a solution. In such cases we usually become more interested in movements from one non-equilibrium situation to another than in a theoretical equilibrium. Suppose, for example, the price of potatoes is relatively low this year because of a bumper crop.

The result may be to induce farmers to plant fewer potatoes now; but when the harvest comes there will then be so few potatoes that the price jumps to a very high level. Farmers are then induced to plant a lot of potatoes and the following year's bumper crop brings the price down again. In other words, there is a time lag between the reaction of supply to price, and we may get a cycle of disequilibrium prices, high and low, in alternate years without reaching equilibrium at all. In circumstances when there are feed backs with time lags in the adjustment process, economists employ more complicated dynamic models, wherein all the variables are 'dated'. These models emphasise the time paths taken by the variables, rather than the equilibrium solutions of the models.

ii. *Stock and flow variables*. Economic behaviour is often related to two quite distinct kinds of independent variables, which we have called **stocks** and **flows**. For instance, the amount a person spends on consumption in a year may be affected by how much money he has in the bank; and also by how much income he earns each year. The former is a stock. It is a quantity of money existing at *any moment of time*. The latter is a flow—income *per period of time*. Of course, the two may be related. For example, if a burglar steals £100 of my stock of savings, I may be induced to spend less this year simply in order to rebuild my assets, even though my annual income is quite unchanged.

## Mathematical models in economics

We deal now briefly with the formulation of economic models in mathematical form. In one sense, we have already started to do so,

Table 9.1   **A demand schedule**

| Price (£) | Quantity demanded |
|-----------|-------------------|
| 8,000 | 0 |
| 5,000 | 1,500 |
| 3,000 | 2,500 |
| 0 | 4,000 |

for a graph is one kind of mathematical formulation. But when economists talk of mathematical models they do not usually mean graphical ones, nor do they mean models specified in arithmetical tables, yet this is another way of expressing a model. Consider, for example, the behavioural assumption on which Figure 9.3 is based. We may recognise it as a demand schedule, which might be summarised in Table 9.1.

Similarly, other lines or curves could be constructed by listing a number of price quantity relationships, though they would be no more than approximations, since it is impossible to list *all* the infinite number of combinations implied by a single curve.

This last defect does not apply to an expression which takes an algebraic form. We do not have space in this book to go into a more detailed explanation of mathematical models. They are frequently considered frightening by students, but this fear may be allayed by the realization that mathematics is simply a different language from English, but which can be shown to mean identical things. Thus, instead of writing 'The quantity of houses demanded depends on the price of houses', we can write:

$$D_h = f(P_h)$$

We are simply using a kind of shorthand in which the meaning of the notation must always be specified. In this case: $D_h$ stands for the demand for houses; $P_h$ stands for the price of houses; $f$ is a mathematical symbol in common use, standing for 'is a function of' and is synomymous with 'is dependent on'.

If the demand for houses was dependent on several factors, the advantages of the shorthand notation would, of course, be greater. Suppose the demand for houses depends on: the price of houses, the price of cars, income this year, income last year, the stock of wealth held by the community in the form of bank balances, and the number of families in the population. Then, using appropriately defined symbols we could write the same thing more briefly as:

$$D_h = f(P_h, P_c, Y_t, Y_{t-1}, B, F)$$

Let us now revert to the simple example where we have only two variables to deal with, one dependent variable and one independent one. Not only can we write very generally as before, that:

$$D_h = f(P_h)$$

To specify that demand is the dependent variable, we can also use algebraic notation to express the precise relationship between them. To stick to our previous numerical example, suppose that demand for houses is that portrayed in Figure 9.3—i.e. that demand is always 4,000 minus half the price of houses. We can write this in the form of an equation corresponding also to the line $DD$ in Figure 9.3, as follows:

$$Q_D = 4,000 - \tfrac{1}{2}P$$

Here $Q_D$ stands for the number of houses people wish to buy (i.e. the demand for houses), and $P$ stands for the price of houses. If you are not sure you understand this, try it out. Take a piece of graph paper and draw axes with scales as in Figure 9.3. Assume any value you like for price. Suppose you chose £6,000, then:

$$\begin{aligned}
Q_D &= 4,000 - \tfrac{1}{2}P \\
&= 4,000 - \tfrac{1}{2}(6,000) \\
&= 4,000 - 3,000 \\
&= 1,000
\end{aligned}$$

Plot the point $P = 6,000$, $Q_D = 1,000$ on your graph. Then take another point. Let the price be, say, £2,842. Then:

$$\begin{aligned}
Q_D &= 4,000 - \tfrac{1}{2}(2,842) \\
&= 2,579
\end{aligned}$$

Plot now the point $Q_D = 2,579$, $P = 2,842$. Join the two points to make a line. Extend the line, and you will find it cuts the price axis at 8,000 and the quantity axis at 4,000.[4] In other words you have drawn the same line as in Figure 9.3.[5]

There is a great deal that can profitably be said about the use of algebra in economics,[6] but we shall have to be satisfied with two important points:

i. *Measuring slopes of curves*. It is possible to infer the slope of a line immediately from the equation describing it. We know that the slope (or gradient) of the line $DD$, for example, tells us how much quantity demanded varies for a change in price—the steeper the curve the less change in quantity for a given price change. But this is precisely the information given by the number preceding the $P$ in the equation $D = 4,000 - \tfrac{1}{2}P$. $-\tfrac{1}{2}$ is said to be the price coefficient, and it tells us by how much to multiply a price change to find the associated change in quantity demanded. $-\tfrac{1}{2}$ is the slope of the line. Note only that when we have relationships in economics which are not linear, this

4. The point at which the line on the graph intersects the axis (where it has the value of the constant term; here 4,000) is called the *intercept*.

5. As an exercise you might try to find the equations for the curves in Figure A.4, (i) to (vi) in the Appendix, pages 211–13. Check your results against the following: (i) $Q = 4 - \tfrac{1}{2}P$, [CD]; $Q = 4 - P$, [HD]. (ii) $Q = 4 - \tfrac{1}{4}P$. (iii) $Q = P$, and $Q = 1\tfrac{1}{2}P$. (iv) $Q = -4 + 1\tfrac{1}{3}P$. (v) $Q = 3 + 1\tfrac{1}{4}P$. (vi) $Q = 6$.

6. See R. Morley, *Mathematics for Modern Economics* in this series.

means that they are true curves with varying slope. We cannot find their slopes algebraically by simple inspection, but only through the development of algebra known as the differential calculus.[7] Alternatively we may derive the slope at each point on a curve on a graph by drawing tangents to it.

ii. *Solving equilibrium models with algebra.* Since each line or curve can be expressed in the form of an equation, we can find the point of intersection of any two lines on a graph without actually drawing them. What is needed is to find the values of the variables that are mutually consistent with each other—in other words the solution of the system of equations. The method used is that for solving simultaneous equations.

Let us take the 'marble model' of Figure 9.2 described on page 185 as an example. We can write $A$ for Adam's marbles and $B$ for Bill's. Then the behaviour assumptions become:

i. $A = 2B$ (Adam has twice as many marbles as Bill)
ii. $B = 21 - 3A$ (Bill has 21 marbles minus 3 times the number which Adam has)

The simplest way of solving this system[8] is, probably, to substitute equation (i) in equation (ii), which becomes

$$B = 21 - 3(2B)$$
$$B = 21 - 6B$$
$$7B = 21$$
$$B = 3$$

And by putting $B = 3$ in equation (i) we get: $A = 6$.

Similarly we could solve the economic model of Figure 9.3 described on page 187, by writing the equations of the curves

$$Q_D = 4,000 - \tfrac{1}{2}P$$
$$Q_S = 1\tfrac{1}{2}P$$

which gives us an equilibrium price, when $Q_S = Q_D$, of:

$$1\tfrac{1}{2}P = 4,000 - \tfrac{1}{2}P$$
$$2P = 4,000$$
$$P = 2,000$$
and  $Q_D = Q_S = 3,000$

7. See Morley, *Mathematics for Modern Economics.*
8. For rigour, it should be added that the method requires that the model should have the same number of equations as there are unknowns.

## Why mathematics?

The introduction of mathematics into economics is sometimes resisted, partly because it makes the subject appear more difficult than it is, and partly because of a feeling that it seems to make human actions appear more predictable than they really are.

The last point is hardly a good one. The value of a model depends on how well it stands up to tests when applied to the real world, not on whether it is expressed verbally or algebraically. Mathematical tools are, today, accepted techniques of advanced analysis. The reason for their acceptance is that the world is a very complex place. Economists need to work with a great number of variables if they are to analyse realistically all the possible interactions of prices and incomes in several markets at the same time. Verbal argument is extremely difficult because we can hardly retain all the variables, and the way in which they interact, in our heads at the same time. Geometry too is ruled out. It is hard enough to work in three dimensions; quite impossible in four or more.

When we set out our hypotheses in algebraic form, there is, in principle, no limit to the number of variables that we can incorporate in the analysis at the same time. If we know what assumptions to make about human behaviour, we can draw a curve, or write an equation to represent them. The better mathematicians we are, the more equations, and the more complicated equations, we can use to build up a relatively sophisticated model economic system in which we can analyse the interactions between several variables at the same time.

Of course, there can be a danger if we waste time manipulating mathematical models in which the behavioural assumptions are wrong. And if we were to forget that our model is only a model, and allow ourselves to think of it as representing the real world, inexcusably erroneous conclusions might be drawn. But this is no more than saying that we must be as sure as possible that we have the right assumptions. Hence the importance of confronting models with facts about the real world, and of drawing our assumptions about economic behaviour with the greatest possible care.

## Model testing

As explained earlier, the gathering of evidence from the real world plays a double role in the method of economics. In one, it provides the basis upon which a theorist may decide how to specify his model, helping him to decide which variables to include and which to exclude. In the other, and at a later stage, it can be used to test the usefulness of the model as a predictive device. These two aspects are not entirely separate, as we observed, since a new model may be built upon results from testing an old one. We may simplify the discussion, however, by imagining that we are concerned with testing the results of a model which attempts to explain an economic event, such as the consequences of a change in the price of onions.

## Making the model testable

Before we can start to confront a model with relevant evidence, we must first make sure that it is in a form that can be tested. Three important checks are needed:

  i.  The model must be positively expressed.
  ii. The terminology used must be appropriate and clear.
  iii. The model should preferably be put in precise quantitative terms.

i. *Positively expressed.* We have discussed this point earlier. There is little use in looking for evidence to support a theory that income tax is too high, or that the rate of economic growth is too low. These are moral, or value, judgments and are right or wrong according to personal subjective preferences. Note, however, that one can often turn a normative statement like 'income tax is too high' into a positive one, which may be tested.

Thus, if we are given a criterion for making an assessment—e.g. that a tax must be judged according to whether or not it decreased the incentive to work—we might construct a model, based on assumptions about human behaviour, to analyse the interactions between these two (and other relevant) variables. It now no longer matters whether the economist thinks it is a 'good thing' or a 'bad thing' for taxes to be lowered or raised. We have a positive statement which seeks only to establish whether tax changes have any effects on work incentives, not whether they may or may not be desirable.

ii. *Terminology.* It is hardly surprising that one should insist on the proper use of language in a model, and it may seem almost unnecessary to emphasise it. But we do not always realise how imprecise a vehicle the English language is for expressing ideas, and how imprecision can give rise to errors in scientific work.

Consider an example from the world of physics. How straight is a straight line? Unless a precise definition of what is meant by straightness is given, one may easily form the wrong conclusion from an apparently scientific experiment designed to see whether or not light travels in a straight line. The answer depends on how straightness is defined. Light travels in waves. These appear if we measure its path over distances shorter than a wave length. Over longer distances the waviness may not be noticeable, and if our observation points are very far apart the results may be misleading.

The social sciences, including economics, are probably even more susceptible to errors of this nature than are the physical sciences. A closely paralleled example in economics can be drawn from research into the relationship between income and consumption. This may be quite different in the short run and in the long run.

To illustrate by extremes, a man does not usually spend every penny he earns each week. Sometimes he saves a portion, sometimes he spends more than his income, as he does when he uses past savings or borrowed money to buy an expensive car or house. Yet over a man's lifetime the tendency for his expenditure to match his income is much greater. Hence, unless we define both income and expenditure precisely with respect to a time period, we can be misled about the nature of the relationship that exists between them.

Economists have created their own vocabulary of jargon, to try to avoid ambiguities in the meaning of words, and value-loaded terms like 'overfull employment'. Many words have technical meanings to an economist, though they are often the same as are used in everyday speech. You have met some in the course of this book (e.g. investment, money and rent) and you must watch out for others. Unless you understand the precise meaning of the words in the theory that you are going to test, you will not be able to interpret your results.

iii. *Quantitative models.* The final check before testing a theory is to try and make it quantitative. You may notice the word 'try' here. Quantification is desirable but not essential, as are Checks (i) and (ii). The reason is obvious. A quantitative theory is more useful than a qualitative one.

For example, we know more about the economy if we can be reasonably confident that price changes are accompanied by, say, 2 per cent changes in the opposite directions in demand, than if we merely know that price changes lead to inverse changes in the quantity demanded. However, many qualitative models may still be useful. Quantification, which raises their value, may come after empirical work has been done by way of testing. Hence Check (iii) is different in nature from Checks (i) and (ii).

## Laboratory experiments

We assume, now, that we have a model ready for testing. Suppose it is the simple one that the demand for salmon increases by $x$ per cent for every fall in the price of salmon of $y$ per cent, where $x$ and $y$ stand for real numbers. Our object is to ascertain the influence of one independent variable (price) on a dependent variable (quantity demanded) in circumstances where we have no doubt that there are many other factors—such as income and tastes—which affect the demand for the commodity, salmon. The problem is to make allowances, somehow or other, for all of the potential influences.

The most effective procedure would be to control all but one of the explanatory variables—to hold them constant and unchanged (*ceteris paribus*) while we varied price. If we were conducting a laboratory experiment in the physical sciences this might not be so difficult. Physical forces can usually be controlled in the laboratory. Suppose we wanted to find out the determinants of some physical event; e.g. what causes a liquid to change into a gas? We know that at least two factors, heat and pressure, are involved. We are actually able to provide conditions of constant pressure in a laboratory while subjecting a substance to changing heat. We can, in general, design an experiment to observe the effects of one variable on another, holding other determining variables constant (*ceteris* truly *paribus*). Moreover, we can repeat an experiment over and over again to see whether we get similar results each time; and we gain confidence in the results the more often they are confirmed.

In the social sciences, repetitive controlled experiments are regarded as rarely possible, because people react in a laboratory in a manner which may be quite different from the way they would react in a real situation. It is difficult to hide from people that they are taking part in an experiment, however it is arranged. Once they realise that they are being treated as guinea pigs, they may try to show off their 'best' (or 'worst') behaviour. Moreover, it is hard to imagine many experiments taking place on a large scale, since economists would obviously never be allowed to tamper with wages, prices, taxes, etc., simply in order to test their latest theories. Occasionally experiments may be made, but all suffer from the signal disadvantage that they are virtually unrepeatable under identical conditions; and they cannot conceivably be used to trace *all* the potentially interesting relationships between variables that the economist needs to study. The economy is simply too complex.

## Statistical analysis of economic behaviour

The social scientist is therefore denied the advantage of the controlled, repeatable laboratory experiment. He is forced to turn for his evidence to actual behaviour of human beings in uncontrolled conditions. But things are changing all the time in the real world, and if the economist has powerful enough tools he can identify important associated variables, like prices and quantities, which regularly move together. For example we cannot deliberately alter peoples' incomes for experimental purposes, but we can identify groups in various income brackets and observe, as we did in Chapter 1, how they allocate their expenditure on different goods and services.

The tools which the economist uses are those of statistical analysis, and their application to economic events is so specialised a task that a new branch of the subject known as econometrics has been developed to cope with it. We shall not enter into a technical discussion of statistical methods here. The essence of econometrics lies in a search for regular, stable patterns of behaviour, which can be reasonably expected to continue. If, for example, it is always found that consumption expenditure rises by 75 per cent of any rise in income, we would regard this as being a consistent behaviour pattern. We should be able to say that there was a high degree of *correlation*, or *association*, between the two variables. We might even honour their relationship with the title 'law' though we should not by that term mean that we considered it to be in any sense inviolable.

## Kinds of evidence

The raw data with which the econometrician must work are the statistics which he can obtain from public and private sources. They can often be deployed graphically with advantage as we have done throughout this book.

One of the most useful kinds of graph is that known as a **scatter diagram**, which can suggest pictorially whether there is any clear pattern of association in the behaviour of any two variables in which one is interested. Suppose we want to find out if there is any association between the lengths of individuals' thumbs and those of their big toes. We take these measurements from, say, 25 people, and for a start we plot them in a scatter diagram on graph paper, as in Figure

9.5. We measure the toe length on the vertical axis and thumb length on the horizontal one, so that each point on the graph represents both measurements for a single individual. Thus point $A$ may refer to Andrew, who has a thumb of 2 inches and a big toe of $1\frac{1}{4}$ inches.

The scatter diagram depicted in Figure 9.5 suggests certain characteristics of the relationship between the two variables. They appear to be positively correlated, and we can even make an estimate of the average association between them. This we can do by imagining a line drawn on the graph which indicates the average trend for

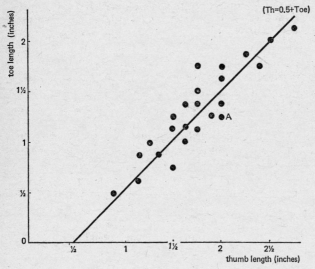

*Figure 9.5*

all 25 people taken together. This, the **line of best fit** (as it is called), can be drawn by eye, or with statistical techniques which need not concern us.[9]

In Figure 9.5 the line has been fitted by eye. It is straight, though there is no reason why a curve should not be fitted if the scatter of points suggests that that would be a better way of portraying the association. The line itself suggests that, on average, people with 2-inch thumbs have $1\frac{1}{2}$-inch toes, those with $2\frac{1}{2}$-inch thumbs have 2-inch toes, etc. In the language with which we are familiar, the

9. One of the most common techniques is known as least squares. The line of best fit drawn in such a way is that which minimises the sum of (the squares of) deviations from it by all individuals.

line has a slope of $(+)$ 1 in 2, i.e. an increase of '$X$' in thumb size is associated with $+ \frac{1}{2}X$ in toe size.

## Confidence in the relationship

How reliable is the 'rule' about average relationships of toes and thumbs that we have just discovered? This question raises two main issues:

i. The association revealed in the diagram is much more reliable for large numbers of people than for single cases. If we know that one man has a thumb of 2 inches, we are quite likely to be wrong if we predict that he will have a $1\frac{1}{2}$-inch toe. But suppose we have 100 men with 2-inch thumbs, we are much more likely to be correct if we forecast that the average size of their toes is $1\frac{1}{2}$ inches. This is because we have some idea of individual variation in our scatter diagram. If you look at the four men shown on the graph with 2-inch thumbs, no single one happens to have a $1\frac{1}{2}$-inch toe, but the average of all four is $1\frac{1}{2}$ inches.

What is true for personal measurements is no less so in economics. If, for instance, we want to estimate the response of consumers to a change in the price of a good, we are much more likely to be correct in a forecast for a large number of consumers, than for a single one of them. Incidentally, we may note that this way of looking at facts gives the lie to the common objection to attempts by economists to measure social reactions—that human beings are too fickle to be able to reduce their behaviour to mathematical rules. The objection would be a very strong one if economists were concerned to predict individual behaviour. It is scarcely so when the job of the economist is directed at finding patterns in the average behaviour of large numbers of individuals—as, of course, it is.

ii. The confidence one can have in any apparent association depends, secondly, upon the scatter of observations around the line of best fit. Figure 9.6 shows two scatter diagrams which might be compared with Figure 9.5. The line of best fit in the left-hand graph, Figure 9.6(i), is almost certainly less reliable, because the spread shows wide variations between individuals. The line in the right-hand diagram, Figure 9.6(ii), is deserving of less confidence because the number of observations is small and even though they lie exactly on a straight line, one would not be very happy deriving a general rule from so small a sample of persons.

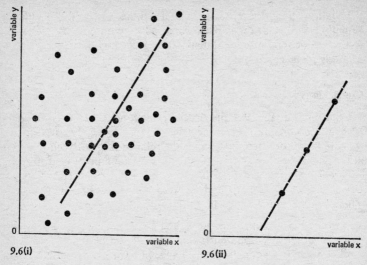

Figure 9.6

## Testing probability

One way of describing degree of confidence, or lack thereof, is by considering the possibility that a particular result could have occurred purely by chance. Statisticians have developed ways of estimating the **probability** that a result could have occurred at random. Their measures are based upon the amount of scatter and the number of observations, and a convention is adopted of accepting probabilities of 1 chance in 20, or 1 in 100, as benchmarks. If a relationship between, say, price and quantity is shown to have odds of less than 1 in 20, or 1 in 100, of having occurred simply by chance, the observed pattern is described as being **'statistically' significant.**

The benchmarks are useful, though somewhat arbitrary ones, because they convey some criteria for judging whether any associations between variables discovered by economists might be due to pure chance. We must never forget that the term statistically significant has a technical meaning, which is quite different from real significance. We may sometimes be justified in paying scant regard to a result which appeared, nevertheless, to be statistically significant by conventional criteria, if we have grounds to suspect it—e.g., because the data, though the best available, were of doubtful quality. Equally, we may at times place some reliance on a result which, on test, was not shown to be statistically significant, but we had other grounds for accepting it.

## Conclusions from a test

We consider, finally, the question of what conclusions may be drawn from the confrontation of a model with evidence. Let us suppose that we have collected data about the relationship between two variables and that they consist of the observations portrayed in either Figure 9.5 or Figure 9.6. We have found the line of best fit indicating the average relationship and wish to draw our final conclusions. There are three aspects to be considered:

i. Whether the fit is a good or bad one.
ii. Whether any apparent association is causal.
iii. Whether the conclusion is a specific or a general one.

i. *Goodness of fit.* (*a*) *Bad fits.* If the scatter is wide, and (or) the number of observations small, the line of best fit may still be a poor one. We must conclude that no firm relationship between the two variables has been demonstrated: any hypothesis based upon the data cannot be said to be confirmed. But it does not necessarily follow that no relationship exists, only that none has been shown. If only a limited amount of data was available, the exercise might be worth repeating. A lack of an apparent association between variables, on the other hand, may have been caused by the data not being suitably defined. Suppose, for example, an association has been sought between expenditure on durable household goods and family size. Here one would be faced with the question: how long should a good last before it is considered durable? Houses, cars, cameras are obviously durable, but what about light bulbs, pencils, ink, tinned food, tomatoes, ice cream? Where should the line be drawn? There is nothing absolutely durable or perishable about any of these things. Hence, one must consider whether redefining the term 'durable' could not perhaps alter the result significantly, and reveal a closer association between the two variables.

A possible explanation of the failure of an expected relationship to be confirmed by the evidence is that the model used was too simple. While statistical techniques may usually hold effectively constant all the variables included in the model, sometimes the techniques break down. Moreover, as has often been emphasised the world is a very complex place and we cannot include every single potential explanatory variable in the analysis. Some exogenous (outside) variable may have changed and disturbed the results.

Suppose, for instance, that we used a model to examine the relationship between the price of houses and the quantity demanded, but excluded the level of income from consideration. In other words, other things were not equal (*ceteris non paribus*). The price of houses might have risen over the period covered by our data; but no fall in demand might have been observed, because incomes rose at the same time.

(*b*) *Good fits*. If we have a relatively large amount of factual evidence, and the scatter about the line of best fit is small, we may be sufficiently encouraged to believe that the hypothesis that we tested is correct. However, even the presence of apparently supporting evidence must be treated with caution. Just as one can be unlucky with the sample data used, but may not necessarily reject a theory which seems to be contradicted by the evidence, so one may be lucky, and by chance use sample data which appear to support a hypothesis. The only safe conclusion that may be justified is one that treats a hypothesis as apparently in accord with the facts as observed —not as proving it correct.

Moreover, even if the theory is indeed correct, it may not always be of predictive value if the model on which it is based is incomplete. For instance, it is said that a better than random way of predicting tomorrow's weather, even in Britain, is to use a model which says that tomorrow's weather will be the same as today's. The predictive value of this hypothesis is apparently good *on average*. Yet it cannot forecast a single one of the important *changes* in weather that occur.

ii. *Causal relationships*. Perhaps the most important danger to avoid in drawing conclusions from statistical evidence is that of assuming that an apparently high correlation means that one variable necessarily *causes* changes in another. In the first place, the reason for the high correlation may be related to the point previously made—that there is an important exogenous variable which is the true cause of the association. For example, there is a high positive correlation between the numbers of suicides and of marriages, but no one seriously believes that the relationship between them is causal. Each happens to be highly correlated with the size of the total population, which is increasing. In this case, it is obvious that the correlation is not causal, but by no means all false causation is so obvious as this example, and we should always be on the look-out to avoid making mistakes of this kind.

Even if a causal link does exist, one may have difficulty in deciding which variable is the cause and which the consequence. For instance, rising wage rates are positively associated with rising prices, but although correlation may be known to be causal, we still want to ask which of the two is the independent variable. We may even wonder whether there is a single answer to the problem, or whether at some time wage rates cause rising prices, while at others the rising prices are the cause of the rising wage rates. Perhaps the answer is neither of the variables, but that there is a 'chicken and egg' relationship between them, each causing a change in the other.

Usually it is easier to identify the causal of two associated variables if we know the times when they occurred—i.e. whether one always preceded the other. But even then there is a trap, and we must be careful to avoid committing a *post hoc ergo propter hoc* kind of fallacy. ('After the event therefore because of the event.') A cautionary tale to illustrate this danger comes from experiments into incentives made by an American, Elton Mayo, in the inter-war years. His team of researchers was particularly interested in the causes of high productivity stemming from personal work effort. Administrative changes were introduced in a factory to improve working conditions, and rates of pay were raised. Each improvement was followed by an in-increase in productivity, and the temptation to infer a causal connection between the two was very strong. Fortunately, Mayo's team made the experiment of reversing the administrative improvements. Amazingly, worsening the conditions and lowering wages did not lead to lower productivity. They produced still higher effort!

The moral of the story can be pointed without going into the reasons for the apparent paradox.[10] It is: be cautious about attributing causes to high statistical correlation. Nothing is ever finally, conclusively and eternally proved in the social sciences. It is often easier to make measurements than to know exactly what it is that you are measuring. So we should be well advised to adopt a reasonably sceptical attitude to statistical evidence, and to go on testing.

iii. *Generalising the results of tests.* The last matter to consider in drawing conclusions from the results of testing hypotheses by con-

10. The explanation runs in terms of the workers responding to interest being taken in them regardless of detailed administrative changes. For an interesting account of the Hawthorne experiments see J. A. C. Brown, *The Social Psychology of Industry*, Penguin Books, 1954, Chapter 3.

fronting them with factual evidence is: how far one may safely generalise from a particular piece of research. There is little guidance of a general kind to be given here. Each case must be treated on its merits and left to the judgment of the individual.

However, one particularly dangerous trap that awaits the beginner who wishes to draw general conclusions from the results of individual experiments, is worth mentioning. It is known as the **fallacy of composition**. If a statement is correct for each and every member of a population, it is not necessarily correct for the population as a whole.

For example, at a noisy party, each individual will be more easily heard if he shouts a bit louder. But if everyone does so, the benefit to each individual cancels out. No one may be better heard. Indeed the din may get so loud that no one can be heard at all.

There are a number of important examples of this kind of trap in economics. For instance, each individual breakfast cereal manufacturer may be able to sell more of his product if he increases expenditure on advertising. But we cannot assume that if all cereal manufacturers increase advertising expenditure together, total sales will rise by the sum of the increases of all individual manufacturers' expenditure. The extra sales of each may be achieved only at the expense of others, and total demand for breakfast cereals may be constant.

Another example of the fallacy of composition was discussed in Chapter 7. It is the so-called paradox of thrift. The reader may remember the argument here, which is that we cannot conclude that an increase in the propensity to save for every individual in the economy will mean that total savings increase (see pages 132–4).

### The end product: 'Economic laws'

We have come to the end of this discussion of the methods used by economists to build models and test their conclusions against the evidence of the real world. After seeing some of the problems involved, it should hardly be surprising that economics has not produced as many reliable laws as the physical sciences. The validity of 'economic laws' is, in practice, difficult to establish, and they are probably better described as tendencies—the *tendency* for demand curves to slope downwards, or the *tendency* for consumption expenditure to increase as income rises. Such 'laws' are useful only in so far as they are supported by evidence. They do not necessarily apply in every individual case; they may not be reliable in the ever-changing environment of a real economy; and they are in no sense, of course, inviolable.

Predictions concerning economic behaviour are, for the same reasons, liable to error. People sometimes scoff when economists turn out to be wrong, especially when economists make contradictory predictions. No one should imagine that forecasting is easy, as meteorologists and doctors, for example, may witness. But, the development of new techniques; and the availability of powerful computers, which can subject great quantities of data to detailed analysis, bring hope that predictions in economics will continue to improve. To end this chapter with a value judgment, the more accurately we can predict the future the better we can control the economy to prevent or alleviate its less desirable features.

# Appendix

# The meaning and use of graphs in economics

A graph is a pictorial representation of the relationship between (normally) two variables. It is drawn on squared paper, on which two vertical lines are drawn, known as axes, which intersect at a point called the origin. Each axis is divided by a scale into units. Along each of these, quantities of a variable are measured.

Figure A.1 is a graph which has been prepared to show the rela-

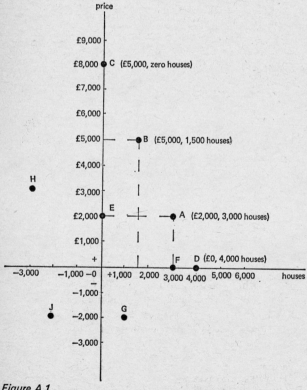

*Figure A.1*

tionship between two variables—the price of houses and the number that people wish to buy (i.e. the demand for houses). Let us measure price on the vertical axis, and numbers of houses on the horizontal.[1] (*Never* forget to label axes on a graph, and you will be saved from many errors.)

Next let us set the scales so that 1 cm = 1,000 houses, or £1,000. Then any point on the graph describes one particular quantitative relationship between houses and prices. Consider the point marked $A$. To find out what quantities are indicated at $A$ we need only drop perpendiculars to each axis. $AE$ tells us that the price indicated by point $A$ is £2,000; $AF$ that the number of houses is 3,000. In other words, if we wanted to convey that 3,000 houses would be bought at a price of £2,000, we could merely stipulate point $A$ on the graph.

Similarly, point $B$ represents 1,500 houses at a price of £5,000.

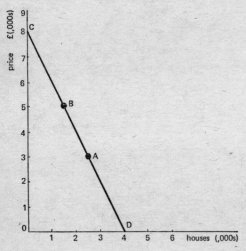

*Figure A.2*

Point $C$ represents no houses and a price of £8,000. Point $D$ represents 4,000 houses at a price of (£) zero. It would also be true to say that $G$ represents 1,000 houses and a negative price of *minus* £2,000; and that $H$ represents *minus* 3,000 houses and a price of £3,000, etc. But because the last points involve negative numbers of houses or

1. Students of mathematics may be shocked to hear that economists sometimes refer to straight line relationships as demand 'curves', and that the positions of the dependent and independent variables are conventionally reversed.

prices, they have no real meaning and can be ignored, as can all points in the three quadrants of the graph other than the one 'North-East' of the origin which shows only positive values of both variables.[2]

Suppose, however, that we wish to represent not just one or two relationships between prices and quantities of houses, but a whole continuous behavioural set. We do this in Figure A.2, which reproduces the relevant part of Figure A.1, except only that the convention has been used of writing (£,000s) after the word price, which labels the vertical axis. This convention allows us to abbreviate each of the numbers on the axis, so that 1 stands for £1,000; 2 for £2,000, etc. A similar simplification is adopted for the scale on the horizontal axis.

We now wish to show graphically the associations between prices and quantities over a whole range of each. This we do by drawing a line on the graph, such as $CD$ on Figure A.2. We infer from this line that the number of houses which people want to buy is to be read off the graph for any price by dropping a perpendicular to the horizontal axis. It is a very brief and economical way of describing the full relationship, which could, in principle, also be described by listing every single price and quantity combination on the graph ($A$, $B$, $C$, $D$, etc.).

### Lines, curves, and slopes

We can draw any line on a graph to represent the way in which we believe (or our model assumes) that price and quantity are related. The line $CD$ on the graph is said to show a *negative* (or inverse) *linear relationship*. This means only: (*a*) that when price changes the quantity is assumed to change *in the opposite direction* to the price (i.e. it is negative); and (*b*) that when price changes by a given absolute amount from any given starting point, the quantity always changes by a uniform amount (i.e. it is linear).

There is, naturally, no need to make either of these assumptions if they are not true. But much economic analysis is in fact worked with models which make the assumption of linearity because in many cases it happens to be useful as a first approximation. The word linear is self-explanatory, but it is worth trying to understand why a relationship in which changes in one variable always produce uniform changes in the other will obviously be a straight line on a graph.

An intuitive grasp of the reason can be obtained from Figure A.3. We assume that point $J$ lies on a line $JV$. This line represents a price

2. The other quadrants are used in more advanced work.

quantity relationship in which a change in price of 1 always leads to a change (in the opposite direction) of 5 in quantity. Let us start from point *J* (price 16 and quantity 20), and move along the line to *L* (price 15 and quantity 25). In other words, we assume price falls from 16 to 15 and quantity rises from 20 to 25.

The movement from *J* to *L* is, in fact, a downhill slide along a hill

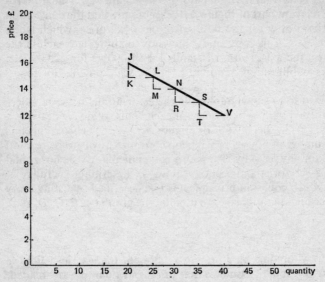

*Figure A.3*

with a certain slope. To measure this slope, we may imagine that we first descend vertically by *JK* and then move horizontally by *KL*. The relationship between the height *JK* and the length *KL* *is* the slope.

If price were to continue to fall in steps of one unit (by *LM*, *NR*, *ST*, etc.) exactly the same increase in quantity would recur—5 units (= *MN* = *RS* = *TV*). In other words, the slopes of the line between *L* and *N*, between *N* and *S*, and between *S* and *V*, are all the same as the slope between *J* and *L*. This property of common slope of the line *JV* still applies if price falls by 4, from 16 to 12. The quantity rises by 20 (5 times 4) since the slope of *JV* is, of course, the same as the slope of its constituent parts.

You may never have thought that a straight line is one with a constant slope, but a moment's reflection should convince you. If a line starts to bend this means that its slope changes. Hence, the logical conclusion that JL has a constant slope really means also that the line is a straight one.

An alternative way of looking at the argument is to recall the standard manner of describing a slope or gradient of a hill—as 1 in 10, 1 in 5, etc. These ratios imply, of course, that a hill goes perpendicularly up (or down) 1 foot (or whatever unit we like to measure in), for every 10 (or 5) feet horizontally that we travel. A straight line such as *JV* is like a hill with a constant gradient—*JK* in *KL* etc., or 1 in 5. If the slope were to change, the line would no longer continue to be straight. You may like to see for yourself what happens if the slope changes by moving further downwards from *V*, assuming that a price change of 1 leads to a change of 10 in quantity. Compare the extension you must make to *JV* with what would occur if you continued to assume that a unit change in price leads to a change of 5 in quantity.

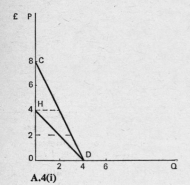

A.4(i)

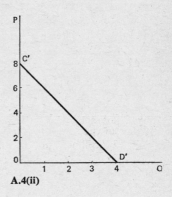

A.4(ii)

You should now have a basic idea of the meaning and use of graphs, but you may like to exercise your understanding by looking at a number of graphs portraying different relationships between variables.[3] Let us examine briefly those in Figure A.4(i) to (xiii), each of which shows the association between price and quantity:

(i). The line *HD* shows a negative relationship with a less steep slope than the original *CD* in Figure A.2, which is redrawn for comparative purposes on the same graph. From the new curve we can infer that a given change in price causes a larger change in quantity. If price falls

3. See also the very full explanation in R. Morley, *Mathematics for Modern Economics*.

from say, £4 to £2, the quantity rise is 2 on *HD*, whereas it is only 1 on *CD*.

(ii). *C'D'* is a line which shows an identical relationship between price and quantity to the original *CD*. We are, however, using a different scale along the quantity axis. *C'D'* and *CD* have exactly the same slope, although it does not appear to be the same. We should take this as a warning not to judge a slope on sight, without looking carefully at the scale of a graph

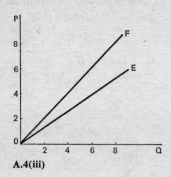

A.4(iii)

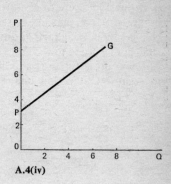

A.4(iv)

(iii). The lines *OE* and *OF* show two *positive* linear relationships be-tween price and quantity. Price changes are always accompanied by changes in the same direction as quantity changes. The two curves differ only in their slopes. (Can you say at once which implies that a given price rise will lead to the larger quantity increase?) The two lines have, however, an important common property arising from the fact that they both start at origin *O*. If price changes by a given amount, quantity always changes by a uniform amount regardless of the absolute level of price (and vice versa).

(iv). *PG* is similar to *OF* and *OE* in (iii) in that it shows a further positive linear relationship between the two variables. They differ however in one important respect. Whereas the lines *OE* and *OF* show that quantity is zero when price is also zero, *PG* shows that quantity is zero even when price is positive—in fact at *OP*. A techni-cal way of distinguishing *OG* is to say that the line intersects the price axis, instead of going through the origin. (*OP* is, in fact, called the *intercept*.)

(v). *QJ* is similar to *PC* of (iv) in that it is both positive and linear, and does not go through the origin. However, *QJ* intersects the quantity axis rather than the vertical price axis. The implication to be drawn from $QJ$ is that a positive quantity is associated with a zero price ($OQ = 3$).

(vi.) $KL$ shows yet another linear relationship with a slope which is neither positive nor negative, but zero. $KL$ implies that price and

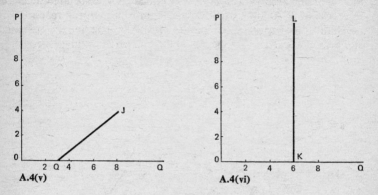

A.4(v)  A.4(vi)

quantity are not associated. A change in price does not cause any change in quantity.[4]

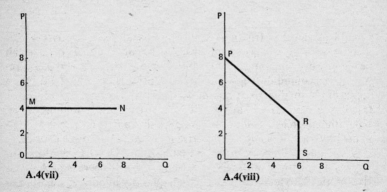

A.4(vii)  A.4(viii)

(vii). $MN$ shows a linear relationship with an infinite slope—the exact opposite of $KL$ in (vi). If you find this hard to imagine, try thinking of the original line $CD$ in (i) becoming continually less

4. If we changed the convention and for once put price on the horizontal and quantity on the vertical axis, the slopes of the lines in (vi) and (vii) would *look* more like the way in which they are described.

steep. A given price change then causes a continually larger increase in quantity. When the line becomes horizontal, the increase in quantity accompanying even a tiny price fall is infinitely great.

(viii). *PRS* is a combination of *C'D'* in (i) and *LK* in (vi). The line indicates that price and quantity are negatively associated at prices in excess of 3. At prices below this, saturation point is reached and no change in quantity accompanies price falls. The line has no single slope, but a negative slope on the *PR* portion, and a zero slope along *RS*.

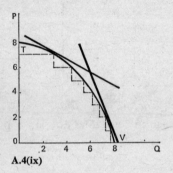
A.4(ix)

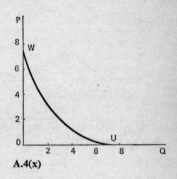
A.4(x)

(ix). *TV* is the first true curve. Its slope is always negative, but it increases numerically as we move down the curve from *T* to *V*, as can be seen by drawing tangents at arbitrary points along it. *TV* could represent a demand curve, where a fall in price is accompanied by an increasingly smaller rise in quantity the lower is price.

(x). *WU* resembles *TV* in (ix). It is also curvilinear and negative, but with a decreasing slope. *WU* implies that a fall in price is accompanied by an increasingly *larger* rise in quantity the lower is price.

(xi). *OA* and *OB* are positive and curvilinear. On *OA* the slope increases as we move up the curve, and on *OB* it decreases. A given rise in price is associated with a rise in quantity in both cases, but the rise in quantity decreases as price rises on *OA* and increases on *OB*.[5]

(xii). *OL* shows a further curvilinear relationship between price and quantity which starts by being positive, but becomes negative after point *L*.

5. (N.B. A curve of similar shape to *OA* could illustrate graphically the hypothesis of page 1 that the demand for houses varies with the square root of their price.)

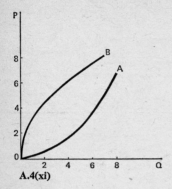

A.4(xi)

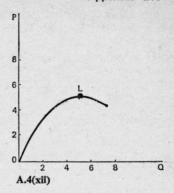

A.4(xii)

(xiii). *BEH* is a particular type of negative curve which has special economic significance. Its peculiar feature is that a given *proportionate* change in price is always accompanied by an *equal proportionate* change in quantity. In this respect it is the negative counterpart to

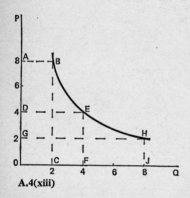

A.4(xiii)

positive curves through the origin *OE* and *OF* in (iii). Curves such as *BEH* have a special name, *rectangular hyperbolas*, by which they are sometimes known (even in economics), because the area of rectangles enclosed by dropping perpendiculars at points on the curve to the two axes are always equal—*OABC = ODEF = 16*).

# Index

References given in heavy type indicate the main source